The

KINGS & QUEENS

of England & Scotland

The
KINGS &
QUEENS
of England &
Scotland

MARIA COSTANTINO

© 2010 Kerswell Farm Ltd

This edition published by King Books

Printed 2012

This book is distributed in the UK by
Parkham Books Ltd
Barns Farm, Boraston
Tenbury Wells
Worcestershire
WR15 8NB

david@kingbooks.co.uk

ISBN: 978-1-906239-33-6

DS0174. Kings & Queens of England & Scotland

Creative Director: Sarah King
Editor: Sally MacEachern
Project editor: Judith Millidge
Designer: Jade Sienkiewicz

Printed in Singapore

3 5 7 9 10 8 6 4 2

CONTENTS

THE FIRST ENGLISH KINGS: SAXONS, THE HOUSE OF WESSEX, DANES AND VIKINGS

75 BC–AD 20

The islands that make up Great Britain have been inhabited since the last ice age, and for the past 3,000 years – or maybe even longer – the hierarchical social structures that emerged encouraged the development of chieftains who ruled over small agrarian communities. In the 8th century BC the first wave of Celts arrived in Britain from mainland Europe, eventually settling in Ireland and on the Isle of Man. A second wave followed in the 5th century, this time bringing advanced iron making techniques, horses and wheeled vehicles, and soon a significant tribal structure was formed, with the chiefs as the dominant 'aristocracy'. From 75 BC and for the next hundred or so years, Celts arrived from Gaul: the Belgae settled in Kent, the Atrebates in Hampshire and Sussex, the Parisii in Yorkshire with other tribes – their sworn enemies – like the Iceni settling in Norfolk, the Dubunni in Cornwall, the Silures and Ordovices in Wales and the Marches, the Brigantes in Yorkshire and the Trinovantes in Essex. These tribes were all independent of each other, and each had its own 'king'.

In 58 BC the Roman general Julius Caesar decided to rid Gaul of the remaining Belgae tribe, many of whom fled to Kent. In 55 Caesar assembled a huge fleet and an army of 100,000 cavalry and infantry, and set sail in pursuit, only to find it difficult to land on the coast. A second campaign followed the following year, and after a series of skirmishes, the 'British' were forced into an encampment guarded by wooden stakes on the north side of the River Thames. Recognising the strength of the Roman army, the 'chief of chiefs' of the Britons, Caswallon, negotiated with Caesar who took tributes and hostages before returning to Gaul.

Ninety years later, the Romans would return, but in the meantime, the social structure in Britain allowed for the emergence of Cunobelin – the Cymbeline of Shakespeare's play – and one of the most powerful kings of the ancient British who, by AD 20, controlled a kingdom stretching from the north bank of the Thames across the southeast of England.

Julius Caesar was the first Roman emperor and his name became a royal title. For over 2,000 years after his death there was at least one European head of state entitled kaiser or tsar.

The Roman invasions ended the rule of Iron Age chiefs in Britain during the first century AD.

Despite the former glories of the Roman occupation, by 388 AD Britain was no longer part of the Roman Empire.

Son of the Catuvellaunian king, Cunobelin, Caractacus fought a guerrilla campaign against the Romans.

Hadrian's Wall marked the northern limits of the Roman Empire.

Boudicca, who died in AD 60, led the Iceni of East Anglia in revolt against the Romans.

AD 43–AD 410

In AD 43 the Emperor Claudius appointed Aulus Plautius to organise an invasion of Britain. Landing in Kent, the Roman army swept inland and engaged Caratacus (the heir of Cunobelin) in the battle of the Medway. The Romans were victorious and chased the Britons to a ford on the River Thames. Caratacus fled to the west while Claudius remained at the river crossing where he received homage from eleven chieftains. A bridgehead was built at the ford: this was Llyn-Din – 'the hill by the pool' – or what the Romans would call Londinium. A strategically important site, London, as it would become, was accessible by ship but far enough inland to make it relatively safe from attack by sea. Claudius would never return to London but from Rome he established the first governorship of Britain under Plautius, although it would be another 30 years or so before the Romans fully conquered Britain.

Famous among the resisting tribal chiefs was Boudica, queen of the Iceni, who in AD 60 rose in revolt in her legendary chariot. At first successful in defeating the Roman army at Colchester,, Verulamium (St Albans), and Londinium (London) Boudicca's army met the main Roman force returning from Wales. Although greater in number, the Iceni were no match for the disciplined Roman army and after intense fighting, the British were defeated. For the next 350 years, Britain was to remain a colony of Rome and subject to a series of governors.

Few of the emperors came to Britain, but those who did left their mark, notably Hadrian who in the summer of AD 112 began building the famous Hadrian's Wall to mark out the extent of Roman territory – and to keep out the warring Picts from Scotland. At 73 miles (117 km) long (and taking four years to build), Hadrian's Wall also marked the most northern limit of the Roman Empire.

In the 4th century AD Britain began to gain some notional independence from Rome as an increasing number of emperors were declared in the country. The most famous of these was Constantine the Great (306–37) who made Christianity the official religion in Britain and furthermore divided the country into four provinces: Britannia Prima (Wales and the west Country); Britannia Secunda (the north); Flavia Caesariensis (the Midlands and Norfolk) and Maxima Caeseriensis (the south of England), with four regional capitals at Cirencester, York, Lincoln and London.

Soon though, Britain was coming under attack from the Picts in the north, from the Franks and Saxons in the south-east (they had landed in 367 and laid siege to London) and the Irish in the west and although Rome sent more troops, by 388 they had more or less abandoned the province. By 410, Roman law ceased to apply in Britain.

AD 410–AD 731

With the collapse of Roman rule, warfare spread across Britain: new chiefs emerged such as Coel (the 'Old King Cole' of the nursery rhyme) who dominated the territory from York to the north to the rivers Forth and Clyde for some 40 years. The Dark Ages in the southern parts of Britain saw a number of local rulers including the 'legendary' King Arthur. And by the middle of the 5th century, Saxons, Jutes and Angles from northern Germany began raiding and then settling in the land. Over the next 200 years, the invaders pushed the natives Britons into Scotland and Wales and set up kingdoms of their own: by the 7th century England was divided into the seven warring kingdoms of the Heptarchy: Kent, Susses, Essex, East Anglia, Wessex, Mercia and Northumbria.

VIKING RAIDERS AND THE FIRST KING OF ENGLAND

The first raids by the Vikings on Britain occurred in 787 and for the next two centuries continuous raids threatened the coasts and the people of Britain. The Vikings were not entirely successful as each of the Heptarchy kingdoms kept them at bay before turning on their neighbours to try and gain supremacy. Kent and Northumbria fought to convert their neighbours to Christianity, (the religion brought to England by St Augustine in 597). Northumbria was the first of the kingdoms to become the most powerful but it was overtaken by Mercia. After the death of Offa in 796 (who constructed the 150 mile long earthwork stretching from the River Dee to Tidenham on the River Severn to protect his kingdom from the Welsh), the kingdom of Wessex emerged triumphant and in Ecgbehrt, king from 803–29, produced the first King of England.

THE 'NOT-SO-DARK' DARK AGES

It was not all warring and killing in this period: the Anglo-Saxon era in Britain was also a time of great scholarship and produced some of the finest pieces of art. It was once thought that the Anglo-Saxons did not build in stone – the presumption was that they were lacking in masonry skills and were probably too busy fighting to engage on complicated or large-scale projects. But with the advance of Christianity from the 7th century, many churches and some small cathedrals were constructed. Of the examples that have survived, the tower and turret of Brixworth Minster in Northamptonshire dating from the mid-8th century, and St John's Church at Escomb in County Durham from around the same period are fine examples of Anglo-Saxon skill and craftsmanship. In 731 the Venerable Bede, an English monk and historian who spent most of his life in the monasteries at Monkwearmouth and Jarrow in Durham, completed his *Ecclesiastical History of the English People*, which began with a short description of Celtic Britain and outlined the events of the Roman occupation.

King Arthur was probably a 6th-century king in western Britain, not the romantic hero from legend.

Viking raiders attacked Britain for over 200 years, until King Alfred agreed peace in 878.

The Lindisfarne Gospels, one of the finest Anglo-Saxon illuminated manuscripts, was produced at Lindisfarne Priory in the 8th century.

King Alfred (r. 871–899) led England against the Vikings.

Canute (r. 1016–1035) was one of the most successful early medieval kings.

Westminster Abbey was built by Edward the Confessor. The abbey was consecrated in 1065, shortly before the king's death.

The monastery at Lindisfarne off the north east coast of England was also famous for its beautiful illuminated manuscripts. In 1939, the fabulous remains of the burial ship of Raedwald of East Anglia (c. 600–617) were discovered in a trench near the River Deben at Sutton Hoo in Suffolk. The ship contained armour, coins, ceremonial wear and jewellery that demonstrated the wealth of the Anglo-Saxon king and the considerable technical and artistic skills of workmen at the time.

ALFRED THE GREAT 871–899

The greatest of all the Wessex kings – and the only English king to be called 'the Great' – was Alfred (r. 871–899) who, from his capital at Winchester, spent much of his early reign fighting the Vikings. In 878 after routing their army, Alfred signed the Treaty of Wedmore with the Viking leader Guthrum, dividing England along a line running northwest from London to Chester. Alfred ruled the southern part but was also recognised as overlord of the area to the north, known as the Danelaw. But further Viking invasions followed and in 886, Alfred captured London and was finally accepted by both Danes and Saxons alike as king of all England. He codified and reformed Saxon law and sponsored the compilation of the *Anglo-Saxon Chronicles* that were written in Anglo-Saxon, the language spoken by the people, rather than in Latin, the language of the Church. The *Chronicles* outlined the political, social and economic events in England and were continuously updated until the 12th century. Alfred himself also translated from Latin into Anglo-Saxon Bede's *Ecclesiastical History of the English People* and St. Augustine's *Soliloquies*.

CANUTE 1016–1035

After Alfred died in 899 the powerful kingdom of Wessex continued its domination of England. First under Alfred's son Edward the Elder (899–924), and then his successors, by 975 the Danes had largely been expelled from Britain, but under the weak kingship of Ethelred II (978–1016) the invaders were being 'paid off' with Danegeld rather than seen off with the sword. Ethelred II was known as the 'Unready' or more correctly, the 'Redeless' because he refused to take advice and in 1013, the Danish king Sweyn Forkbeard seized the opportunity to invade and pillage much of the country. So, when Ethelred died in 1016 England found itself with two claimants to the throne: the English chose Ethelred's son Edmund Ironside, while the Danes chose Swyen's son Canute. After several battles with no winner emerging, in 1016 they agreed to divide the country between them. Edmund died soon after and Canute became king, adding England to his vast Scandinavian empire that included Denmark, Norway and southern Sweden. Canute's reign was marked by great prosperity and by good governance:, although a Viking, Canute treated Dane and Saxon alike and wisely appointed Englishmen to positions of power in the Church and at his court. He also married Ethelred's widow, Emma, Countess of Normandy in 1017. Once again the country was divided, this time into four earldoms of Mercia, Wessex, East Anglia and Northumberland.

ANGLO-SAXON KINGS

1035–1066

EDWARD THE CONFESSOR 1042–1066

After Canute's death in 1035, his son Harold ruled with cruelty and abandon (according to the *Anglo-Saxon Chronicle*), until his death in 1040. Harold was succeeded by his half-brother, Harthacanute, who was king until 1042. The *Anglo-Saxon Chronicle* reports that Harthacanute failed to do 'anything worthy as a king while he reigned'. When he died, Edward the Confessor (son of Ethelred the Unready) was 'elected' king. Born in c. 1003, Edward was pious but strong, and was determined to govern the country with a firm hand. He sought to control the growing power of the earls and banished the rebellious Godwine, Earl of Wessex (although he allowed him to return in 1052), and raised fleets to see off the Vikings. He did, however, make enemies, largely because unlike Canute who strategically placed Englishmen in power, Edward showed a preference for Norman-French advisors. In one of the great controversies of history, Edward apparently promised the English throne to his kinsman William, Duke of Normandy in 1051. In 1064 Harold Godwineson, the son of the expelled earl of Wessex, who was now the advisor and brother-in-law to Edward, visited the court of William of Normandy and swore an oath to support his claim to be king.

THE BATTLE OF HASTINGS

Edward the Confessor died in 1066 without an heir and successor. Fifteen years earlier he had promised the throne of England to William, Duke of Normandy, but on his deathbed reneged on his promise and bequeathed the throne to his brother-in-law, Harold Godwineson, who became king as Harold II. Incensed by this betrayal, on 28 September 1066, William landed unchallenged at Pevensey Bay on the south coast of England with the largest fighting force since the Roman invasion. Although the Norman Conquest would be the last foreign invasion of England until 1688, in 1066, England was attacked by two enemies. At the time of William's arrival, Harold's army was occupied with repelling a Viking force at the battle of Stamford Bridge in Yorkshire, 300 miles away. A few miles inland from Hastings, William built a castle and awaited the arrival of the exhausted English army that had beaten back Harald Hardrada. On 14 October at Senlac Hill, (the battlefield, as well as the magnificent Norman abbey can still be seen at Battle just north of Hastings) 7,000 Norman troops fought and defeated the army of the Anglo-Saxon king Harold II. Now hailed as the 'Conqueror', William lost no time and marched his victorious troops through the countryside, subduing any resistance en route to London. By December 1066, King William I had been enthroned at Westminster Abbey, the first in the line of England's Norman monarchs.

This scene from the Bayeux Tapestry shows the critical point at the Battle of Hastings, when King Harold was fatally injured by an arrow to his eye.

THE NORMANS
1066–1154

The Normans were themselves originally Vikings (or 'Norsemen', men from the north) who had settled in north-west France in the early 10th century under the leadership of Rollo the Ganger (c. 860–932), who sailed up the River Seine to Rouen and then besieged Paris in 886. Baptised and granted the provinces of Normandy by King Charles 'the Simple' III of France, Rollo was the first duke of Normandy until his retirement to a monastery in 927. The Viking instincts of the Norman dukes encouraged them to seek new lands to conquer and to settle: in the 11th century they expanded outwards from Normandy and conquered both southern Italy and England. During the 11th century, links between Normandy and England were strong. Edward the Confessor's mother was Emma, sister of Robert, Duke of Normandy and members of the royal family, including Edward himself, were educated in the duchy. It is not surprising, therefore, that he appointed many Frenchmen to positions of power within England.

REBELLIONS AND DANEGELD

Having won a decisive victory at Hastings, William's control of England in the early years of his reign was restricted to the south of the country and part of the midland Saxon kingdom of Mercia. Soon though, William began to consolidate his gains and in February of 1067, confident of his authority and rule, left England for a nine-month visit to Normandy. In charge in England was William's half-brother Odo, Bishop of Bayeux and the Norman baron William FitzOsbern. It was on William's return in May 1068 that resistances to Norman rule turned into rebellion: Harold's sons raided the south-west of England from their base in Ireland, seizing Exeter after a two-week siege, and in 1069 the Danes, supported by Edgar the Aetheling (who had been nominated as heir to the throne by his uncle, Edward the Confessor), invaded the north and captured York.

There were rebellions, too, in the Midlands and under the Saxon ruler Hereward the Wake, uprisings in East Anglia. Meanwhile the Scots and the Welsh were causing trouble on England's borders. William acted swiftly and decisively: the Viking invaders were paid off with Danegeld; the Marcher lordships were created on the borders of Wales and given to William's most trusted barons (including FitzOsbern) to rule as they saw fit, and, in 1069, he began the Harrying of the North, a period of what can only be called genocide, across the country between York and Durham. In 1071 East Anglia was subdued following the Siege of Ely, after which William put pressure on Malcolm III, King of Scotland, forcing him to sign the Treaty of Abernethy that marked a truce between the two kingdoms. The Norman military conquest of England was now complete and William could turn his attention to governing the country.

THE NORMANS

1066–1154

NORMAN RULE

England in the 11th century was an agrarian economy. Although over the previous centuries, the Anglo-Saxons had settled in villages and cleared large tracts of woodland, there were still great forests and areas of moor lands with millions of acres not under the plough. When the Normans arrived, they set about changing both the landscape of England and they way the land was governed: laws were introduced to protect the forests, which at the same time, restricted access to hunting in them to the nobility. Any man – or dog – found hunting in the forests could be 'hambled' (his hamstring would be pulled and the trespasser left crippled for life). Under William's successors, more than half of England was designated as royal hunting forest and the Norman 'forest laws' became extremely unpopular. Monumental churches were built or rebuilt, and French and Latin became the official languages of the land. The previous rule by Anglo-Saxon nobles with their 'moots' (meetings) and the Witenagemot or Witan (an early parliament, in which the most important members of the monarch's court met to discuss state and foreign affairs and to advise the king) was replaced by a feudal system. Norman barons became the king's 'tenants-in-chief' of the old manors, whereby instead of paying rent, the barons were obliged to provide knights for the king's service. In turn, the barons themselves sub-let their new manors and land, passing the obligation down the social scale until the poor became no more than serfs, obliged to serve as soldiers when required, to work their feudal lord's land without pay for a number of days every week, and to pay a percentage of their own produce from their portion of land to the feudal overlord every year.

THE DOMESDAY BOOK

For most of the 1070s and early 1080s, the 'government' of England was left in the hands of the powerful barons – in particular Richard Fitzgilbert and William de Warrenne – while William the Conqueror was occupied with his continental territories in Normandy. In 1085, William returned to England with a huge army to defend the country from a planned invasion by Canute IV of Denmark. Canute was assassinated before the invasion began and William was left with a restless army that needed paying. It was vital that he raised money, but the real problem was knowing who owned what lands and what they were worth so he could tax them. The solution was to survey England to record land ownership and usage. The survey, completed in 1086 was the Domesday, or Doomsday Book.

Durham Castle was built in the 11th century as a projection of William's power in the north.

The New Forest was created as a royal hunting forest by William I in 1079.

The original two-volume Domesday Book is stored in the National Archives at Kew, west London.

1066–1154

The name comes from the belief that its assessment or 'judgement' was as final as that of the Biblical doomsday on the day of judgement. It consisted of two volumes: one was a survey of the prosperous counties of Essex, Suffolk and Norfolk, and the second volume covered the rest of England (although Northumberland and Durham were omitted, as were London, Winchester and certain other towns). The two volumes provide a record of the extent, value, the state of cultivation, ownership and tenancy of the land, and even recorded the number of livestock in each shire. It noted ownership and value before 1066, and the new owners after the Conquest. It is possible to track William's brutal progress through northern England from the pages Domesday Book. Villages that were prosperous before 1066 are ruined by 1086 as a direct result of the Normans' suppression of rebellion in 1069. Seventeen years after the Harrying of the North, many had not recovered. Furthermore, the Domesday Book recorded the size of the human population that in 1086 stood at some two million people, ruled by fewer than 200 barons.

CASTLES

Perhaps the most visible reminders of Norman rule are the castles that replaced the wooden Anglo-Saxon structures, and in some cases, the town burghs that had been erected to defend the people. The Norman castle was more than a defensive structure: it was a visible representation of power, authority and status and lay at the heart of local government. Castles provided a secure base from which the feudal lords could oversee theirs lands, while inside the walls, the castles housed their families and became the base for local tax collection and for settling local disputes. Soon after the invasion, the Normans began to stamp their authority across England with castles at Cambridge, Warwick, Nottingham, Huntingdon, Lincoln and York.

The first castles were of two types, both with a simple design: the most common type was the motte-and-bailey castle. This consisted of a raised mound of earth (motte) on top of which stood a wooden tower (housing the owner). Around the motte was a wooden walled park (bailey) surrounded by ditches. Windsor Castle in Berkshire began as a timber and earth motte and bailey castle before being rebuilt in stone during the 11th and 12th centuries.

1066–1154

Less common was the enclosure castle: a raised platform of earth surrounded by a wooden palisade and then enclosed by a ditch and a bank. High on the cliffs in Kent, dominating the coast and surrounding countryside, Dover Castle was originally an enclosure castle before being extensively rebuilt.

Like earth and timber castles, stone castles were also of two types. Both were stone walled enclosures, often surrounded by a moat, with various buildings arranged within, but some had a great stone tower at or near the centre, while others didn't. An early example of a Norman stone castle is the Tower of London begun in 1078. Soon after his victory, William sent an advance guard of engineers to London to erect a castle, both as a sign of the new regime, and to prepare for his public and triumphal entrance into his new capital. By 1078 a new stone keep was under construction, and the imposing White Tower itself was complete by 1100. The towers came in a range of shapes and sizes- rectangular, round, polygonal and even D-shaped and ranged in height from 50-100ft (15-30m) tall and 30-100ft (10-30m) across. Stone castles were expensive to construct and slow to build: the average construction time was around 10ft (3m) a year.

In spite of William's ruthless policies and his brutal treatment of resistance to Norman rule, he was respected as a leader. His invasion transformed England forever. England was reduced to a prize of war, the booty promised by William to his knights. By 1086, only two of the Anglo-Saxon tenants-in-chief remained in a position of power – the rest had been replaced by William's Norman followers. So the ruling class of England was swept away and replaced by a French-speaking aristocracy. French became the language of government, and English was spoken by the natives, who, the evidence suggests, were regarded as second-class citizens by the victorious Normans.

After William's death, his successors tightened the grip over both England and France until rivalry between Henry I's daughter Matilda and his nephew Stephen caused anarchy and chaos that ultimately led to the demise of the House of Normandy and its succession by a new French dynasty, the House of Anjou in 1154.

The Round Tower at Windsor Castle was constructed by William I and was intended to guard the western approaches to London.

The White Tower is the original part of the Tower of London and was completed by 1100.

WILLIAM I

1066–1087

William the Conqueror was the illegitimate son of Robert 'the Devil', Duke of Normandy and his mistress, Herleva, the daughter of a burgher of Falaise, called William the Tanner. Since marriages – especially among the nobility – were for political alliance, Duke Robert was married off to a suitable bride in the form of Arlette of Conteville, while Herleva was married to a Norman baron: from this union, Herleva produced two sons, William's half-brothers Robert and Odo who would later support him at the Battle of Hastings.

Despite his illegitimacy, William was his father's only son, and inherited his father's duchy in 1035, aged just seven or eight years old after Duke Robert died on pilgrimage to Jerusalem. A mere child, yet nonetheless powerful, William was the target for many assassination attempts and plots to overthrow him. Managing to survive, by the mid 1040s, William was starting to assert his own authority: in 1047 William's cousin Guy de Brionne rebelled and tried to seize the duchy. Guy had considerable support so William turned to King Henri I of France for help in a tightly fought battle. The king's recognition of William as the rightful Duke of Normandy gave William his authority, while victory in battle no doubt consolidated a ruthless streak which would encourage William to viciously retaliate against anyone who challenged his rule. William now began a campaign of expansion: to consolidate his lands and possessions he married Matilda, the daughter of Baldwin V, Count of Flanders in 1059. While the marriage fortunately also turned out to be a love match and produced ten children, William may also have seen in his bride a further link to his claim on the throne of England: Matilda was a direct descendent of the Anglo-Saxon king, Alfred the Great.

According to contemporary accounts, William was tall, about 5 ft 10 in. (1.8 m) tall, thick-set, red-haired, with a rasping voice. It was said he had a fist that could 'fell an ox' and 'an eye that could quell the fiercest baron'. William was undoubtedly a charismatic leader who commanded and received respect. William's claim on the English throne rested on two points: first, he was a descendent of the Scandinavian earls of Orkney and the great-nephew of Emma of Normandy (the wife of King Canute) and secondly, he maintained that his distant cousin, the childless Edward the Confessor had promised the throne to him and that Harold Godwineson, the most powerful man in England had agreed to support him. Harold had sworn an oath, either of allegiance or assistance to William, after his ship had been blown off course and he had been captured off the French coast. Under pressure from his nobles, the dying Edward the Confessor reneged on his promise. Harold then also reneged on his oath and took the English crown for himself.

William was understandably furious, and true to character, quickly and decisively laid plans to invade England in order to take what he believed was rightfully his. William recruited a vast army of men from Normandy, Boulogne, Brittany, Flanders and Italy: many of the barons and knights who

WILLIAM I 1066–1087

Nicknames: *The Bastard, later the Conqueror*

Dynasty: *House of Normandy*

Born: *Falaise Castle, Normandy, in 1027 or 1028*

Succeeded to Throne: *14 October 1066*

Crowned at: *Westminster Abbey, 25 December 1066*

Died: *Priory of St. Gervais near Rouen, France on 9 September 1087*

Buried: *St. Stephen's Abbey, Caen, France*

Authority: *King of England and Duke of Normandy*

Parents: *Robert I 'the Devil', 6th Duke of Normandy and Arlette of Conteville*

Married: *Matilda of Flanders (died 1083) in 1051 or 1052 in Eu Cathedral, Normandy, France*

Children: *Nine, notably Robert 'Curthose' (c.1053–1134), William II, Henry I, and Adela, (c.1063–1137)*

Pevensey Castle was built by the Romans, and temporarily fortified by Harold, but it was more or less undefended the Normans landed in 1066.

There are no contemporary portraits of William the Conqueror, but according to one eye-witness, he was a robust man, who although sparing of food and drink, grew fat in his later years.

supported William owed him no feudal allegiance but had shrewdly calculated his chances of success and were 'investing' in the prospects for gain in England. In exchange for their support, and importantly, their capital that was needed to finance the invasion, the Norman barons and knights stood to gain control of no less than three-quarters of all English land (with the other quarter to be owned by William).

Nevertheless, the conquest of England was by no means a foregone conclusion: Harold Godwineson's army was one of the fiercest and most disciplined in Europe and included the crack troops of the *housecarls* who were equipped with deadly, two-handed battleaxes. Furthermore, William would have to confront Harold on his own territory. If it hadn't been for the almost simultaneous onslaught by Harald Hardrada of Norway that Harold was forced to fight at Stamford Bridge at the opposite end of the country, in Yorkshire, on the 25 September, England may well have remained under Saxon rule. A victorious but tired and weakened army of some 6,000-7,000 soldiers was forced to march back south quickly to fight William's army that had landed at Pevensey Bay on 28 September. While William waited for Harold's army to arrive, he made the most of his time by building defences and pillaging the surrounding villages and farms – a tactic that drew Harold towards William's army rather than forcing William's army to move away from the fleet at Pevensey and its supply lines.

When the two armies finally met on the morning of 14 October, the English were lined up 10-12 deep on the top of the ridge of Senlac Hill, about six miles inland from Hastings. Just 400 yards (365 m) below, at the bottom of the ridge, were 7,000 Norman troops, nearly half of whom were mounted knights in armour. The Normans attacked first but were beaten back down the ridge: the Saxon soldiers saw their retreat as a sign of a broken line and confusion and charged down the hill after them only to be met by a Norman counter-attack. A second assault on the ridge also failed and the Norman troops fled back down the hill, once again drawing down the Saxons in pursuit. The Normans again turned around and began to systematically pick off the Saxon soldiers using mounted knights and archers. When Harold and his brothers were slain, the remains of the Saxon army submitted to William.

WILLIAM I

1066–1087

Once called William 'the Bastard', he was now William the Conqueror, but although he was to style himself king of England, not all of England accepted his rule, and it was not until 1067 that he was able to begin his systematic conquest of the country. Advancing through the country, William adopted a practice of besieging recalcitrant towns forcing them into submission, building a castle (a total of 78 were built on his orders, the most famous being the Tower of London) and installing a Norman duke or baron to maintain peace in the area and with responsibilities for levying and collecting taxes. In 1068, William's authority was such that he felt it was safe to bring Matilda from France and she was crowned Queen. Matilda remained in England for a little over a year and accompanied William on his 'tours': their last son, the future king Henry I was born at Selby in Yorkshire in 1068. The following year Matilda returned to France where she remained until her death in 1083.

By 1072, William believed his conquest of England was complete: he had paid off the Viking invaders with Danegeld, brought the northern parts of England under his control following brutal and bloody battles, made a truce with the Scottish king Malcolm III and secured the Welsh borders by installing his most trusted and powerful barons as feudal overlords. His conquest complete, William returned to Normandy and did not return for any significant period until 1085 when he came back with a huge army to defend the island against invasion by Canute IV of Denmark, an invasion that never happened. In 1086 William ordered the survey of all England in order that he could establish ownership, tenancy, the extent and value of the land in order to levy taxes on it. The resulting document was the famous two volumes of the Domesday Book. Of this remarkable and highly accurate survey of England, William made little use himself: he was preoccupied with returning to Normandy to quell a local rebellion.

William left for France at the end of 1086: in July the following year as he laid siege to the town of Mantes, where his eldest son Robert 'Curthose' had led a treacherous rebellion. During the siege, William's horse jumped a ditch causing the pommel of his saddle to rip into his stomach. The wound became infected and eventually led to peritonitis. Carried to Rouen in great pain, William lay dying for five weeks until he died in September. His body was taken to St. Stephen's Abbey in Caen for burial, but it appears the tomb prepared for him was too short for his tall body: as attendants forced his body into the tomb, the decaying and swollen corpse of the king burst open and filled the air with such a putrid smell that most fled the scene and only a few remained to complete the burial.

The tomb of William's eldest son Robert Curthose, in Gloucester Cathedral. As the eldest son, he inherited his father's original lands in Normandy. His younger brother, William Rufus, inherited the English kingdom. Robert and William agreed to name each other as heir, with the intention that the two realms would eventually unite under the surviving brother. Robert's absence on crusade at the time of Rufus's death enabled their youngest brother, Henry, to seize the throne.

WILLIAM II   1087–1100

Nicknames: *Rufus ('the Red', on account of his complexion), William the Red, William the Younger*

Dynasty: *House of Normandy*

Born: *Normandy, France c. 1056–60*

Succeeded to Throne: *10 September 1087*

Crowned at: *Westminster Abbey on 26 September 1087*

Died: *near Lyndhurst in the New Forest, 2 August 1100*

Buried: *Winchester Cathedral*

Authority: *King of England with powers over Scotland, Wales and Normandy*

Parents: *William I and Matilda of Flanders, their third son*

Married: *Unmarried*

Children: *None legitimate*

WILLIAM II

1087–1100

Little is known of William II's early life: it is believed he was born sometime between 1056 and 1060, and was the fourth child of William I the Conqueror and his wife Matilda. Following the early death of his elder brother Richard in 1075, the young William took a step closer to inheriting his father's kingdom, and when in 1087 his other brother Robert Curthose betrayed the family and sided with the enemy at the siege of Mantes, William stayed true to his father and was at his side when he died. Robert was passed over as king of England, but was given the title of Duke of Normandy, while William succeeded his father in September of 1087. Thinking it wise to avoid the considerable resentment of his brother, William sailed for England with a letter confirming his father's wishes to give to Lanfranc, the Archbishop of Canterbury and was crowned at Westminster Abbey on the 26 September. The second Norman king of England, William II was nicknamed 'Rufus' on account of his red hair and ruddy complexion – the only physical traits inherited from his father as Rufus was short, stout, spoke with a stutter and was believed to be homosexual. He did however inherit the warrior characteristics that he used to consolidate the Norman rule in England established by his father.

Contemporary chroniclers, most of whom were monks, tended to paint a picture of William Rufus as an unpopular king: he ruled over a dissolute court where it was said the men dressed effeminately (if dressed at all), and showed apparent disdain for all things religious. He angered the clergy by refusing to appoint bishops and abbots so that he could appropriate church lands (and their considerable incomes) for himself. In 1089 Archbishop Lanfranc died and William refused to appoint a successor. He only did so in 1092 when he was ill and believed he was dying, appointing Lanfranc's student and friend Anselm. This was not the end of William's troubles with the clergy. At this time a schism in the Church meant that there were two popes: Urban II in Rome and the 'anti-pope', Clement III, who claimed authority from Ravenna. In 1095 William convened a council to decide who to support, eventually favouring Urban, who had promised that papal legates would not enter England without royal approval – an agreement that William interpreted as marking his freedom from clerical rule, much to the annoyance of Anselm. The relationship between king and archbishop became so difficult that Anselm eventually went into self-imposed exile in 1097 in Rome – and William promptly seized his estates.

With the division of England and Normandy from 1087, many clergy and several Norman barons who held lands in both France and England were confused over the matter of to whom they owed their allegiance – the king or his brother the Duke of Normandy. Many considered Robert Curthose a more suitable king, and this gave rise to the constant threat of rebellion.

In 1088 William Rufus faced his first insurrection, led by his uncle Odo, Bishop of Bayeux. Robert in Normandy was unable to capitalise on his support among the English barons and William swiftly quashed the rebellion, devastating Odo's estates in Kent in the process. A further brief coup led by

WILLIAM II

1087–1100

William's younger brother Henry in 1091 revealed William to be a skilled negotiator: he successfully brought Robert to his side and eventually reached an agreement between all three brothers for their mutual benefit. William even called on Robert to join him in England on an expedition against Malcolm III of Scotland. But the deep-rooted rivalry between William and Robert was only laid to rest in 1096 when Robert joined the First Crusade. To raise money for his army, Robert pledged Normandy to William, which William then ruled as Regent, winning back lands in France that his brother had lost.

In addition to rebellions from within, William also had to keep check on the Scots: in 1090, encouraged by the Saxon prince Edgar the Aetheling, Malcolm III invaded northern England but was soon rebuffed by William who succeeding in renewing the Peace of Abernethy, which he disregarded in 1092 when he seized lands around Carlisle and constructed a castle there. When Malcolm came to parley, William refused to see him and as the furious Scottish king prepared to cross the border back into his kingdom, he was killed by the Normans in the Battle of Alnwick in Northumbria. In a period of violent upheaval against Norman rule, William cleverly orchestrated events in Scotland to his own ends: when Malcolm's brother Donald Blane claimed the Scottish throne, William supported first Duncan II and then Edgar, Malcolm's two sons, in overthrowing Donald. When Edgar finally became king he recognized the support of William but also realised that he was subservient to him.

At the same time William was stamping Norman authority on Scotland, he was also expanding his influence in Wales: William's initial advance against the Welsh king Gruffydd ap Cynan Gwynedd was eventually repulsed in 1094, but a second advance into the principality in 1098 regained much of the lost territory and several of the Welsh princes recognized William as their overlord. In the last years of his reign, William also continued the Norman practice of defensive construction and established a line of castles along the Welsh marches.

By 1100 William Rufus had largely secured his realm. Like his father, William enjoyed hunting and it was a hunt in the New Forest that would end his life. Late in the afternoon, the king was 'accidentally' shot in the back by an arrow apparently fired at a stag by one of his hunting party, Walter Tyrell. Many (especially the clergy) would have been relieved at William's death. Tyrell insisted on his innocence, claiming he was nowhere near the king at the time, but he was nevertheless quickly sent back to France. One man who was close to the scene at the time of the shooting was William's younger brother Henry and many now suspect his part in a plot to seize the throne. William's body was taken by farm cart to Winchester Cathedral and buried in the early hours of the next morning – but not before Henry had ridden quickly to Winchester to commandeer the royal treasury, which he took straight to London. Although there were some official mourners, William's body was buried with very little ceremony beneath the flagstones under the tower: the following year the tower collapsed.

William Rufus died in the New Forest in August 1100. According to the chronicler William of Malmesbury, he was 'not to be lamented by the people, because he suffered their substance to be plundered'.

The Rufus Stone was erected in 1865 and marks the spot where William II was killed.

HENRY I   1100–1135

Nicknames: Beauclerc ('good reader' or 'good scholar'), Lion of Justice

Dynasty: House of Normandy

Born: Selby, Yorkshire in late 1068

Succeeded to Throne: 2 August 1100

Crowned at: Westminster Abbey on 5 August 1100

Died: Lyons-la-Foret, near Rouen, France, 1 December 1135

Buried: Reading Abbey, Berkshire

Authority: King of England and from 1106, Duke of Normandy

Parents: William I and Matilda of Flanders, their fourth son

Married: (1) Matilda (formerly Edith) (1080-1118) daughter of Malcolm III of Scotland on 11 November 1100; and (2) Adela (Adelaide) (died 1151), daughter of Count Godfrey VII of Louvain on 29 January 1121.

Children: Three children by (1) notably William (b. 1103) who drowned in the 'White Ship' wreck in 1120, and Matilda.

1100-1135

By right – and agreement between the brothers – William the Conqueror's eldest son Robert should have succeeded William Rufus as king of England, but he was away in the Holy Land on crusade at the time of Rufus' death. As the youngest son, Henry had been destined for life in the church and received a fine education: his nickname was 'Beauclerc', or 'good reader'. A well-built man, but more placid than either of his brothers, Henry was still quite capable of great cruelty and ruthlessness: it is said that he once pushed a man named Conrad Pilatus to his death from the ramparts of Rouen Castle for breaking an oath of allegiance to him. The tower from then on has been known as 'Conrad's Leap'. When news arrived in England that Robert was returning – and with a new wife – Henry hastily convened a council that elected him king. Robert arrived home to a fait accompli.

As the only son of William I to have been 'born in the purple', that is, when his father was already king, Henry believed he had a legitimate claim to the throne above that of his brother. He was the first Norman king to speak fluent English and he spent the first months of his reign placating the Saxon population. A highly intelligent man, with an opportunistic streak that enabled him to grab the throne, Henry's reign is noted for the legal and administrative reforms that established Anglo-Norman bureaucracy. His administrative reforms ensured that England was efficiently governed during his frequent absences in Normandy.

Obliged to buy the nobles' support, Henry issued the Charter of Liberties in November 1100, which promised to restore the rule of law abandoned during the reign of William Rufus, notably the restoration of the laws of Edward the Confessor, as amended by William the Conqueror. This had the dual effect of earning him popularity with the Saxon population, and endearing him to the barons, whose support was vital. Henry promised good governance, but actually increased the powers of the Crown during his reign.

However, he also introduced a range of reforms, including expanding the system of travelling justices throughout the country, and developed the Curia Regis (King's Council) to settle disputes between the Crown and tenants. These actions gave rise to his other nickname of 'Lion of Justice'. The exchequer was established to administer royal revenue efficiently.

HENRY I

1100-1135

Three months after his coronation, Henry married Matilda (also known as Edith), the sister of the Scottish king, Edgar, thereby cementing an alliance with Scotland, and he arranged further alliances with Flanders and France, just in case brother Robert decided to attack, which he did in 1101. All out war was avoided and Robert returned to Normandy with a settlement of £2,000 a year. But the truce did not last. In 1106 at the Battle of Tinchebrai, Robert was captured and sent to Cardiff Castle under lock and key where he remained until his death in 1134. Robert's death seemed to clear the way for Henry's son and heir William Adelin (born in 1103 and made Duke of Normandy when Robert was imprisoned) to eventually succeed his father.

But in November 1120 William was drowned aboard the White Ship which had been steered on to rocks by a drunken pilot en route to England from Normandy. Although Henry had as many as 20 illegitimate children, his only remaining legitimate child was his daughter Matilda. When her mother Queen Matilda died in 1121, Henry married a second time in 1122 to Adela of Louvain, but this union did not produce an heir. With his options increasingly limited, Henry named his daughter Matilda as his successor, but the death of her husband Emperor Henry V of Germany and her subsequent marriage to Geoffrey Plantagenet of Anjou made this problematic as most Norman and English barons were hostile to the Angevins. This decision would eventually lead to civil war in England.

When Henry died in 1135 in Normandy probably from food poisoning (or from eating a 'surfeit of lampreys', according to legend) his body, sewn into the hide of a bull to preserve his remains, was returned to England to be interred at Reading Abbey which Henry had founded 14 years earlier.

Although it was Henry's daughter Matilda who was named queen, it was his nephew, Stephen, who seized the crown. Henry's death plunged England into chaos and the administrative reforms which had made England a relatively peaceful and well-governed kingdom for 30 years were abandoned as Matilda and Stephen jostled for control and the barons' support oscillated between them.

HENRY I.

Henry I was a skilled administrator who established an efficient system of governance for his empire.

When Henry I's only son, William Adelin, died in the White Ship in 1120, the succession became the key political question for the remainder of Henry's reign.

STEPHEN 1135–1154

Nicknames: none known
Dynasty: House of Blois
Born: Blois, France about 1097
Succeeded to Throne: 22 December 1135
Crowned at: Westminster Abbey on 26 December 1135
Died: St. Martin's Priory, Dover, Kent on 25 October 1154
Buried: Faversham Abbey, Kent

Authority: King of England, Count of Boulogne with claims on Normandy (until 1145)
Parents: Adela (daughter of William I the Conqueror) and Stephen, Count of Bois, their third son.
Married: Matilda of Boulogne (c. 1103–52) the daughter of Count Eustace II of Boulogne, in 1125
Children: Five, notably the eldest son Eustace, Count of Boulogne (c. 1126–53)

1135–1154

Stephen was the third son of Henry I's sister Adela (c.1063-1137), and Stephen, Count of Blois (d.1102). Stephen was a favourite of Henry I, who presented his nephew with great riches and vast tracts of land: it was said that Stephen was the second biggest landowner in England. Such assets made Stephen both rich and powerful, but he also profited from his marriage to Matilda, the only daughter of the Count of Boulogne in 1125. For the next ten years, Stephen remained fiercely loyal to his uncle Henry I, even it seems, when the king named his daughter Matilda as his successor.

Like her cousin, Matilda was a grandchild of William the Conqueror, and as the daughter of King Henry I, Matilda arguably had a stronger claim to the throne. The barons (led by Stephen himself) had sworn loyalty to her, but when Henry died in 1135, it was clear that many of them were not ready for a female ruler. Furthermore, her marriage to Geoffrey of Anjou was unpopular.

When Henry I died in 1135, Stephen seized the crown for himself. Matilda objected, but she was in Anjou at the time, and Stephen had a geographical advantage which enabled him to claim the throne. He also had the support of some very powerful people, not least his brother, Henry, Bishop of Winchester and Pope Innocent II, who recognised Stephens' right to rule. Intelligent, good-natured and well-mannered, Stephen was quite different to his 'ruthless' Norman predecessors. Walter Map who wrote during the reign of Henry II, described Stephen rather damningly as, 'A man of a certain age…hard-working, but otherwise a nonentity [idiota].' The apparent lack of ruthlessness, though, would prove to be Stephen's undoing. The *Anglo-Saxon Chronicle* recounts that very soon, 'the great men who were traitors rose against him. When the traitors saw that Stephen was a good-humoured, kindly and easy-going man who inflicted no punishment, they then committed all manner of horrible crimes . . .'

In 1138 Stephen's kingdoms on both sides of the Channel began to fall into anarchy and chaos. There were skirmishes with King David of Scotland in the north and north-west of England, and with Matilda's husband, Geoffrey of Anjou who had his sights set on taking Normandy. But the biggest threats to Stephen's reign came from Robert Fitzroy of Gloucester, just one of Henry I's numerous illegitimate children, who switched his allegiance from Stephen to Matilda. Stephen then fell out with his own brother, Henry of Blois, (who had thwarted ambitions to be awarded the see of Canterbury) and Ranulf, Earl of Chester, who was enraged when Stephen gave Carlisle Castle to the Scots.

STEPHEN

1135–1154

In 1139, three leading bishops including the powerful Roger of Salisbury, were imprisoned for plotting against Stephen, but to make matters worse, the same year, Matilda arrived in England and was rewarded with growing support for her claim to the throne. Stephen took Matilda prisoner at Arundel Castle, but soon lost his chance to keep control when she was freed and set up a rival court in the west country. Here Stephen thought he could control Matilda, but he didn't count on an uprising in Ely, and Ranulf of Chester seizing Lincoln.

The first clash between Stephen's and Matilda's armies came at Lincoln in February 1141, when Matilda captured Stephen. Imprisoned in Bristol, the king looked on powerlessly as Matilda planned her own coronation. It never took place, however. High-handed, greedy and unpleasant, Matilda was unpopular and support for her in London dwindled. She was driven out of the city before she was crowned in exchange for the release of Matilda's half-brother Robert, Earl of Gloucester. Stephen was freed and restored to the throne and in fact had a second coronation on 25 December 1141 at Canterbury Cathedral. The civil war would rage for another six years and ravaged England as unscrupulous barons took advantage of the chaos to seize lands and build unauthorised castles for themselves.

According to the *Anglo-Saxon Chronicle* the castles were filled with 'devils and wicked men', and that 'never did a country endure greater misery'. Only when Robert Fitzroy of Gloucester died in 1147 did Matilda give up the fight for the crown of England and return to Normandy. Waiting in the wings, though, was Matilda's son, Henry of Anjou. In 1147 he prepared his army to invade England, but could not pay his men so returned home. Six years later, in 1153, Stephen's son and heir Eustace died. Under the terms of the 1153 Treaty of Winchester, it was agreed that Stephen would continue reign for the rest of his life, and that Henry of would succeed when he died. Henry did not have to wait long: less than a year later Stephen was dead at Dover Castle in Kent and Henry of Anjou was crowned king as Henry II. His death ended a tumultuous period, graphically described in the *Anglo-Saxon Chronicle*: 'And so it lasted for nineteen years while Stephen was King, till the land was all undone and darkened with such deeds, and men said openly that Christ and his angels slept.'

King Stephen was taken prisoner by Matilda's forces in 1141.

THE HOUSE OF ANJOU:

THE PLANTAGENETS
1154–1399

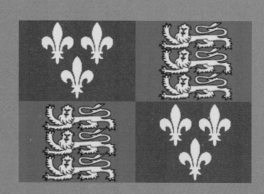

The name Plantagenet is said to have come from a nickname of Geoffrey, Count of Anjou, the father of Henry II: he was said to have worn a sprig of flowering broom – or *Planta genista* – in his hat, a habit which originated when he retrieved his fallen hat while out hunting and at the same time gathered up a handful of the yellow flowers.

England's ruling dynasty for more than 300 years, the Angevin monarchs – of which there were 14 – were spread across different branches of the House of Anjou. The family were nothing if not prolific, and in subsequent centuries, the family tree branched off into Angevin, Plantagenet, Lancaster and York stems, as rulers endowed their sons with suitable titles and lands. King Richard I once said of his Plantagenet family that 'from the Devil we sprang and to the Devil we will go', and the curse of the Plantagents seemed to be that of trying to control ambitious and often unruly heirs.

REFORMS

When the Normans invaded England in 1066, they became the English monarchs. But generations after the Conquest, English monarchs still regarded Normandy as their 'homeland' and used the riches of England to support their campaigns in France to increase their power and lands 'at home'. While the Normans left a legacy of feudal government and monumental buildings like castles and cathedrals, the Angevins monarchs introduced lasting administrative changes into England. Henry II introduced the magistrate system into England's legal process, as well as trial by jury, rather than trial by ordeal. Henry and his successors worked to impose their will on the church and to restrict the influence of the pope. By the Constitution of Clarendon (1164) members of the clergy charged with a criminal offence were to be tried in a civil court, with no appeals to Rome without the king's consent.

1154–1399

THOMAS A BECKET: 'THIS TURBULENT PRIEST'

The Constitution of Clarendon, that limited the power of the Church's jurisdiction over crimes committed by the clergy, did not go down well with many church officials. In 1162 Henry II had appointed Thomas a Becket as Archbishop of Canterbury and charged him to reform the abuses of the clergy. Becket and the king quarrelled violently over the reforms and in 1164, Becket went into exile in France. Reconciled with the king in 1170, Becket returned to Canterbury, but the two soon quarreled again and in exasperation, Henry II is said to have cried out 'Will not someone rid me of this turbulent priest?' Four of Henry's knights took this rhetorical question literally as a command, and on the 29 December 1170, on the high altar of Canterbury Cathedral, they murdered Archbishop Becket.

THE MAGNA CARTA

In 1215 King John sealed the draft of the Magna Carter ('great charter'), now regarded as a milestone in English constitutional history. Drawn up by the senior representatives of the English nobility and the clergy, the Magna Carta was an attempt to curtail what they believed were abuses of royal power in relation to matters of taxation, justice, religion and in foreign policy. The Magna Carta laid down the respective rights and responsibilities of citizens and the church in relation to the power of the throne. The charter limited the king's ability to tax the barons, it guaranteed the rights of the clergy and of city corporations, and held that no free man should be arrested or imprisoned except by the lawful judgment of his peers and the laws of the land.

EARLY PARLIAMENT

Parliament's roots lie in three royal councils: the Anglo-Saxon Witenagenot, or 'Witan', which comprised landowners, bishops, abbots and royal officials; the later Norman Magnum Concilium (Great Council) and later the Curia Regis or King's Court a body of advisors which advised the monarch. In 1265 Simon de Montfort, while in rebellion against Henry III summoned a 'parliament' of his supporters from among the lords, clergy and knights, and most radically, representatives from the town boroughs. In 1295 this composition was adopted by Edward I as the 'Model Parliament'. By the reign of Edward II (1307–27) no laws could be passed or taxes introduced without the consent of parliament. It was divided into two houses, with the Commons occupied by four knights from each shire and two burgesses (citizens) from each borough. This was the first time that all classes of English men – but not women or villains (serfs) –were represented in Parliament.

Thomas Becket window, Canterbury Cathedral.

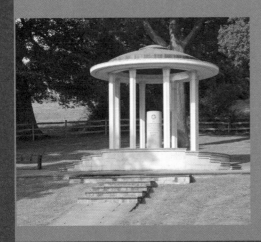

The Magna Carta Memorial, at Runnymede marks the spot where King John was forced by the barons to sign Magna Carta in 1215.

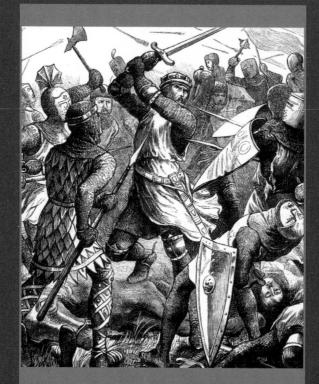

Simon de Montfort led baronial opposition to Henry III. The Battle of Evesham was his last, unsuccessful, stand.

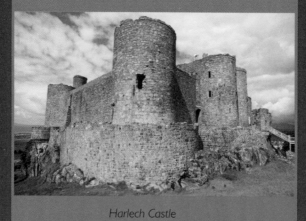

Harlech Castle

THE CONQUEST OF WALES

Driven from England in the 5th and 6th centuries, the Celtic rulers of Wales formed themselves into a number of princedoms that by the 13th century were united and independent of English rule. When Edward I became King of England, the Welsh prince, Llywelyn Yr Ail was summoned to pay him due homage. When Llywelyn refused, in 1277 Edward invaded Wales and imposed English rule.. The English kings then sought to maintain their control over the principality by constructing new castles as the administrative and military headquarters that were strategically sited to command the Welsh coast, river crossings and key roads.

The magnificent castles of Beaumaris, Caernarvon, Flint, Harlech, Rhuddlan and Conway were all initially built over the next 40 years. In 1284 Edward's conquest of Wales was complete and his wife Eleanor gave birth to a son and heir, Edward, while at Caernarvon. According to legend, Edward I held up his new-born son to a gathering of Welsh nobles and declared, 'Here is your new Prince of Wales'. Although the young boy was not formally invested with the title until 1301, since then it has been the tradition for the monarch's eldest son to be created Prince of Wales.

LEARNING AND CHIVALRY

The first universities at Oxford and Cambridge were founded in 1164 and 1209 and the first stone bridge across the River Thames in London was constructed in the 1170s. It was the age in which one of England's greatest poets, Geoffrey Chaucer (c.1340–1400) lived and worked. The Angevin and later Plantagenet reigns were also the period of the Crusades and an era that saw the rise of chivalry. In 1348 Edward III founded the Most Noble Order of the Garter a chivalric order designed to embody the legendary ideals of King Arthur's 'Round Table'. The idea of the order is said to have originated at a dance when the king picked up a garter lost by the Countess of Salisbury and cried out 'Honi soit qui mal y pense' ('Shame on him who thinks evil of it'), fastening the garter around his own leg. (In a lapse of knightly honour, Edward III did, however, ravish the countess one night while her husband was abroad fighting the French.) The Order was – and continues to be – restricted to just 24 people:. Traditionally, Knights of the Garter were members of the royal family, foreign royalty and peers of the realm, but in more recent years, 'commoners' such as Winston Churchill have been honoured as Garter Knights.

1154–1399

SEEDS OF REBELLION:
THE HUNDRED YEARS WAR AND THE PEASANTS' REVOLT

The Angevin rule of England also saw its share of strife: at home there was also widespread discontent among the peasantry of England that erupted into the Peasants' Revolt in 1381. Triggered by the consequences of the Black Death and a series of unpopular 'poll taxes' which taxed each person but was not based on their individual wealth, more than 100,000 men set out from Kent and Essex and converged on London in June 1381, taking Richard II and his government by surprise. Richard met with Wat Tyler of Kent, and Jack Straw and the Essex rebels at Mile End and agreed to the demands of the peasants: an end to serfdom, the fixing of a low rent for all lands, and an unconditional pardon for the rebels.

Once the immediate threat had been removed, Richard withdrew his promises and revoked his pardon, and one by one, the uprisings in the country were violently subdued. Although the Peasants' Revolt failed in the short term, its significance was great: landowners were now reluctant to extract feudal duties from the peasants and soon serfdom would end.

With their strong ancestral links to France, the Angevin monarchs faced spent much of their time embroiled in French affairs. Between 1337 and 1453 England and France engaged in a series of battles known as the Hundred Years War that began with Edward III's claim to the throne of France through his French mother, Queen Isabella. The war can be divided into three phases: first, from 1337–60 which was marked by English success at the battles of Crecy (1346) and Poitiers (1356); secondly, from 1360–1415 in which the English gains were lost to the French; and finally, from 1415–53 which began with Henry V's victory at Agincourt, but ended with the English finally being driven out of France and with France's great prosperity in ruins.

Richard II meets the leaders of the Peasants' Revolt, 1381.

HENRY II

1154–1189

Henry Plantagenet, son of Geoffrey, Count of Anjou and the Empress Matilda, was 21 years old when he became king in 1154. Born at Le Mans in Anjou, Henry was just an infant when he became embroiled in the battle for the English crown that was fought over by his mother and King Stephen. At 14, he made an initial attempt to seize the crown by force, yet a short time later, the ageing king named Henry as his successor on condition that Stephen's own son William would be allowed to retain his titles and estates. On the death of Stephen, the English crown passed unchallenged to Henry II, the first of the Angevin or Plantagenet monarchs, and who also ruled over Anjou, Normandy and Aquitaine (through his marriage to Eleanor of Aquitaine). Strongly built, with the 'head of a lion', red hair and freckles, Henry was athletic and had great energy that allowed him to travel tirelessly across his kingdoms. Throughout his 35-year reign, he was in England for just 14 years.

His generosity to the poor of England, his interest in justice and his reforms of the law to curb the powers of the nobles have led many commentators to describe him as the most able king since Alfred the Great. Through wars and diplomacy, Henry II was master of more of Europe than any other English monarch, and while the later years of his reign were troubled by family revolts, his substantial empire, stretching from the Pyrenees to the Scottish Borders, remained intact. Nevertheless, Henry's long reign was not without its dark passages, most notably the horrific murder of his onetime friend, Chancellor and Archbishop of Canterbury, Thomas Becket, on the high altar of Canterbury Cathedral in 1170. Becket's death was the result of a collision between the powers of church and state, and royal efforts to curb the power of the clergy.

Henry's first task as king was to bring peace to a country ravaged by nearly 20 years of civil war: during the last years of the reign of King Stephen, many of the Anglo-Norman magnates had established their own 'mini-kingdoms' and Henry had to re-establish royal authority. This he did by destroying their hastily constructed castles and taking control of the judicial system that had become regionally varied and overseen by powerful barons. In its place in 1166, Henry established the principles of Common Law – law that was consistent and accessible to all free men in England, with trial by a jury of 12 men and circuit judges in the employ of the Crown (not the Church).

Henry's second task was to reclaim the lands lost earlier to the Scots and the Welsh: successful in the north he reclaimed Northumbria from Malcolm IV and later captured Malcolm's successor, William the Lion. In 1157, Henry sent troops to do battle with the Welsh princes, Owain of Gwynedd and Rhys ap Gruffudd of Deheubarth. In 1155 Henry planned, but postponed an invasion of Ireland that had been sanctioned by the English Pope Adrian IV to bring the 'heretic Irish Church' under Catholic rule. In 1171 Henry finally attacked Ireland and soon the Irish kings acknowledged Henry II as Lord of Ireland.

HENRY II   1154–1189

Nicknames: *Fitz-Empress ('son of Empress Maud'), Curtmantle ('short cloak')*

Dynasty: *House of Anjou/Plantagenet*

Born: *Le Mans, Maine, France on 5 March 1133*

Succeeded to Throne: *25 October 1154*

Crowned at: *Westminster Abbey on 19 December 1154*

Died: *Chinon Castle, near Tours, France on 6 July 1189*

Buried: *Fontevrault Abbey, Maine, France*

Authority: *King of England, overlord of Wales, Scotland, eastern Ireland and western France*

Parents: *Matilda (daughter of Henry I of England) and Count Geoffrey V of Anjou, their eldest son.*

Married: *Eleanor of Aquitaine (c.1122–1204) the daughter of Duke William X of Aquitaine, on 18 May 1152 at Bordeaux Cathedral.*

Children: *Eleven (three illegitimate), notably five sons including his successors, Richard I and John.*

United in death, if not always in life: the tomb of Eleanor and Henry II at Fontevrault Abbey.

Henry II was forced to do public penance for the murder of Thomas Becket.

A chivalric sport, jousting caused the death of Henry II's son Geoffrey in 1185.

1154-1189

While peace had been returned to the land, Henry still faced problems, not least from his own family. In May 1152, Henry married Eleanor of Aquitaine who was as rich, as passionate, as charismatic and, as energetic as him. What should have been a match made in heaven turned into an unhappy marriage. Their first son William was born in 1153 just before Henry was crowned king and did not survive infancy: seven more children were born including four sons. Henry divided his territory between them: Richard would be granted Aquitaine; Geoffrey would rule Brittany, John would reign over Ireland, while the eldest, also called Henry would inherit the English throne along with Anjou and Normandy. To this end Henry arranged a 'coronation' of Prince Henry – the only time an heir to the throne has been crowned during the lifetime of the living English monarch and an event that would bring Thomas a Becket back from exile in France.

It was Henry's reluctance to concede any real control or authority to his sons that angered Eleanor, whose ire was already inflamed by Henry's philandering and his public affair with royal concubine 'the Fair Rosamund' Clifford. Eleanor retired with her court to Poitiers to plot Henry's downfall and the advancement of her favourite son, Richard. In 1173, encouraged by Eleanor, the princes Henry, Richard and Geoffrey rebelled against their father and were backed by the king of France, William the Lion of Scotland and some of the English barons who were outraged at Becket's murder. John appeared to be Henry's only loyal son. Henry crushed the rebellion and placed Eleanor under house arrest but became reconciled with his sons.

In June 1183 Prince Henry 'the Young King', died of fever, and two years later Geoffrey died after an accident at a jousting tournament. Although Henry's kingdom would now be divided between Richard and John, the dynastic rivalries continued. In the summer of 1189 Richard joined forces with Philip II of France to challenge Henry for the crown of England, and Henry was forced into a humiliating peace. Worse though, Henry discovered his once loyal son John had sided with Richard: it is said that this discovery caused Henry's death just two days later from a massive haemorrhage. The sons for whom he had defended and expanded his empire were absent from his deathbed in Chinon Castle. So too was Eleanor: she would live for another 15 years, having entered the convent at Fontevrault. By fate, this was the Abbey church was where Henry II would be buried and in 1204, where Eleanor was buried alongside him.

RICHARD I

1189–1199

Much of the legend and the great reputation attached to Richard I, or 'Richard the Lion Heart' is questionable: while he was undoubtedly brave and a 'champion of Christendom' against the 'infidels', at the same time Richard had very little real interest in England and none whatsoever in its governance. In his ten-year reign, Richard spent just six months in his kingdom.

As the third son of Henry II, Richard had not expected to inherit the crown. Devoted to his mother, he joined in rebellion with his brothers in 1172 after she had been 'imprisoned' (she was under house arrest for a large part of the last 15 years of Henry's reign) in an attempt to achieve greater authority. Richard's greatest love in life was to fight: in his youth he had trained as a knight and was a champion at the tourney. His courage became legendary across Aquitaine where he was duke and where he spent several years crushing rebellious barons. Said to be tall, strong, and handsome, with reddish-yellow hair, Richard attracted as much attention from the men of his court as from the ladies: there is almost certainly some truth to the claim that England's king was bisexual.

On his brother Henry's death in 1183, Richard found himself heir to the throne. When his father died in 1189, Richard travelled from France to England to be crowned – pausing for a while in Normandy to be acclaimed duke. Two years earlier, Saladin's forces had captured Jerusalem and the cry went up across Europe to recapture the city and heart of Christendom from the infidels. Richard's one ambition was to lead an army against the Saracens and his stay in England after his coronation was brief but long enough to raise money and resources for the Third Crusade (1189–92). This included the famous 'Quitclaim of Canterbury' whereby Richard sold all the rights in Scotland back to William the Lion for 10,000 marks. He further sold state and church offices and lands, as well as charters of self-governance to towns. He even offered to sell London if a buyer could be found. With money in his pocket, Richard set sail for France in December 1189 and would not set foot in England again for four years. In his absence, the administration of England fell to William Longchamp, a capable chancellor, but one with a short temper and arrogance that set him at odds with many of the other barons.

Allied with Philip II of France, Richard set off for the Holy Land in 1190. The vast fleet over-wintered in Sicily where Richard's sister Joanna was the recently widowed queen and Richard was unhappy with her treatment by the new king, Tancred. Consequently, Richard captured the town of Messina, which he used to bargain better conditions for Joanna as well as funds for the Crusade. In the meantime the English and French kings were arguing over Richard's betrothal to Philip's sister Alys: the pair had been 'engaged' for 20 years, but it was pretty certain she had been Richard's father's (Henry II) mistress. Richard was determined not to marry her. Matters were further complicated with Richard's mother Eleanor of Aquitaine arrived in Sicily with a new bride for her son, Berengaria of Navarre.

RICHARD I 1189–1199

Nicknames: *Coeur de Lion (Lionheart)*
Dynasty: *House of Anjou/Plantagenet*
Born: *Beaumont Palace, Oxford on 8 September 1157*
Succeeded to Throne: *6 July 1189*
Crowned at: *Westminster Abbey on 3 September 1189*
Died: *Chalus, Limousin, France on 6 April 1199*
Buried: *Initially at Fontevrault Abbey, Maine, France (his heart buried in Rouen); later reburied in Westminster Abbey*

Authority: *King of England and ruler of western France.*
Parents: *Henry II and Eleanor of Aquitaine, their third son*
Married: *Berengaria of Navarre (died after 1230), the daughter of King Sancho VI of Navarre, on 12 May 1191 at the Chapel of St George, Limassol, Cyprus.*
Children: *An acknowledged illegitimate son*

Regarded by many historians as a bad king of England, who simply taxed the country (the so-called 'Saladin tithe') to fund his crusading campaigns, Richard was undoubtedly an expert military leader. In 1192 Richard and Saladin agreed a truce after three years of fighting.

Richard I's reputation has fluctuated over the centuries. He was regarded as a hero by the Victorians who erected this statue outside the Houses of Parliament.

Philip was outraged and hotfooted it to the Holy Land. It was clear to all but the blind that Richard had absolutely no interest in the 'fair sex', but the throne required an heir and successor. In April 1191, Richard (with sister Joanna and bride-to-be Berengaria in tow) set sail, but the ship the two women were travelling in was nearly captured by Isaac Comenus, a rebel Byzantine who had seized power of the strategic island of Cyprus. Ready for a fight, Richard did battle and won Cyprus, which true to form, he then promptly sold to Guy de Lusignan, the exiled 'King' of Jerusalem. With Cyprus safe, Richard married Berengaria – and promptly left her there. Not surprisingly, there were no children from this marriage (it appears Richard preferred Berengaria's brother Sancho) but Richard did father an illegitimate child in his youth with a lady at court in Aquitaine. In 1191 Richard finally reached the Holy Land, where he helped Duke Leopold of Austria and Philip of France win the battle of Acre. But Richard soon fell out with Leopold and he wasn't on particularly good terms with Philip anyway.

Leopold and Philip returned to Europe and Richard killed the prisoners taken at Acre before marching down the coast to Jaffa. Without the military backing of Leopold and Philip, Richard could not take Jerusalem and was forced to conclude a truce after three years of fighting with Saladin. En route for Europe in October 1192, Richard's ship was caught in a violent storm and was wrecked in the Adriatic. Forced to continue his homeward journey by land, he had to cross into Duke Leopold's lands. Disguised – rather badly it seems – as a humble woodsman, Richard betrayed himself by his exquisitely made gloves and his fine manners, and was handed over to the Emperor Henry VI of Germany who demanded a ransom of 100,00 marks for the English king's release.

For the next 15 months Richard was held prisoner in Germany, during which time, according to legend, his minstrel Blondel travelled from one castle to another in an attempt to find him, singing Richard's favourite songs until the king sang back in response from the castle at Durrenstein. The task of negotiating Richard's release – and to raise the money for the ransom from his English subjects – fell to Hubert Walter, Bishop of Salisbury. Promoted to Archbishop of Canterbury and Chief Justiciar, Walter went on to quash an attempt by Richard's brother John to gain the throne. At great expense, the citizens of England paid for the return of their king, who, when released from captivity in Germany, promptly disappeared in 1194 to fight in France. Here he devoted his remaining years to regaining his lost territories.

King Richard I never set foot in England again: injured by a crossbow bolt during a skirmish at the castle of Chalus in the Limousin, gangrene infected the wound and on 6 April 1199, the Lion Heart died, having designating his brother John as his successor (overlooking his elder brother Geoffrey's son Arthur as heir). Poor Berengaria, who lived for another 30 years, settled eventually in Le Mans: she remains unique in being the only English queen never to have set foot in the country.

JOHN

1199–1216

Henry II's youngest – and favourite – son, John was born when his mother Eleanor of Aquitaine was 45, the youngest of nine children. Although clearly spoilt as a child, John had no immediate inheritance as Henry's patrimony had already been divided among his other children, and so he gained the nickname of 'Sans Terre' or 'Lackland'. Described as being about 5 ft 6 in. (1.65 m) tall, plump around the middle, with a bald head inside a ring of curly black hair, a menacing voice and a reputation for hard work, John also enjoyed his leisure. Chief among his pursuits was hunting, but unusually for any man at the time – even kings – he is said to have enjoyed taking baths.

John was a skilled politician and a forceful administrator, but also one of England's most unpopular monarchs largely due to his cruelty and deceit. When his brother King Richard I left for the Crusades in 1190, John was given territory in France and ordered to stay away from England. But John was determined to rule and attempted to overthrow William Longchamp who Richard had left to govern the country in his absence. John's reign over England saw him live up to his nickname: he oversaw the loss of most of the English-held territories in France, placed incredible financial burdens on the English to the extent that the barons were brought to the point of open rebellion. In 1215 they forced him to sign the Magna Carta which imposed limits on the king's powers.

On Richard's death in 1199, John was accepted as king of England, but his Angevin territories preferred the claim of his 11-year-old nephew, Arthur of Brittany, the son of John's older brother Geoffrey who, arguably, had the stronger claim to the throne. During John's campaigns to win back his French lands, he arranged for the young Prince Arthur to be murdered.

In 1189 John married the heiress Isabella, Countess of Gloucester, and while the union lasted ten years, the marriage produced no children and was annulled in 1200 on the grounds that as second cousins, they were too closely related to be legally married. Shortly afterwards John remarried, this time to the 12-year-old Isabella of Angouleme who had been betrothed to Duke Hugh X of Lusignan. The French king Philip II was outraged: not only had John killed Arthur of Brittany, but he had 'stolen' a bride.

Here was Philip's excuse to do battle and fighting started in 1203: by 1204 John had lost Anjou and Normandy to the French and was forced to return to England. The loss of Normandy, the heartland of the Anglo-Norman empire, was a demoralising blow to the English crown, and this military defeat gave rise to John's derogatory nickname of 'Soft Sword'.

JOHN   1199–1216

Nicknames: *Lackland ('Sans Terre'), Sword of Lath ('Soft Sword')*

Dynasty: *House of Anjou/Plantagenet*

Born: *Beaumont Palace, Oxford 24 December 1167*

Succeeded to Throne: *6 April 1199*

Crowned at: *Westminster Abbey 27 May 1199*

Died: *Newark Castle, Nottinghamshire, 18 October 1216*

Buried: *Worcester Cathedral*

Authority: *King of England, with claims to Scotland, Wales and western France; from 1185, Lord of Ireland.*

Parents: *Henry II and Eleanor of Aquitaine, their youngest son.*

Married: *(1) Isabella of Gloucester (died 1217), on 29 August 1189 at Marlborough, Wiltshire; (2) Isabella of Angouleme (died 1246), on 26 August 1220 at Angouleme, France.*

Children: *Five by (2), notably, Henry III, Richard (1209–72), Isabella (1210–38) and Eleanor (1215–75), plus five illegitimate children.*

JOHN.

King John is famous for plotting and scheming against his brother, for reneging on agreements, and for his brutality, but he is also acknowledged as a skilled administrator. Sadly, his drive for efficiency and aggressive pursuit of taxes such as scutage (whereby feudal dues could be paid with money instead of service), brought him into conflict with the barons whose support was vital.

Magna Carta guaranteed the liberties of free men and attempted to limit the king's power.

King John signing Magna Carta, 15 June 1215.

John inflicted massive taxation on an English population already suffering from the burden of having paid Richard I's hefty ransom as well as suffering from rampant inflation. The clergy, too, were soon at odds with John when he refused the appointment of Stephen Langton as Archbishop of Canterbury. The wrath of the clergy over this and the confiscation of ecclesiastical property led to John's excommunication in 1209 by Pope Innocent III. In 1212, Innocent went further and declared that John was no longer the rightful king of England. The threat of attack by the French forced John to submit to the Pope's and the church's demands. England was effectively a pawn in the Vatican's hands. Back fighting in France in 1214, John was again defeated at the Battle of Bouvines, and in England, the barons were close to revolt. Their sense of grievance had been steadily growing since the start of John's reign because of heavy taxation, the continued loss of territories in France (where many of the barons also held lands) and an overall sense that John was abusing his royal powers in matters relating to religion and justice.

In 1215, the barons closed in on John. Led by Stephen Langton, they drew up a list of demands in Bury St Edmunds and threatened civil war if the king didn't agree to them. John asked for time to consider the demands and a truce was arranged. There was a great deal of wrangling and haggling during the negotiations, but with John at Windsor Castle and the barons based at Staines, a halfway meeting place at Runnymede beside the River Thames was agreed. On 15 June 1215 following a short ceremony, the baron's demands were presented to the king in the form of the Magna Carta. It is one of the most important documents in history as it was the first attempt to limit the powers of a monarch and to protect the rights of the barons and free men.

Once the king's seal had been fixed to the agreement, copies of the Charter were made and sent around England. The English barons who had threatened revolt now renewed their allegiance to the king. Claiming that he had been forced to sign under duress, John reneged on the agreements and rights enshrined in the Magna Carta and civil war broke out:. The English barons welcomed Philip of France's son Louis into England who quickly gained control of the south-east of England and captured the Tower of London in May 1216. Forced to take flight, in October of the same year, John was heading north to Lincoln when many of the crown jewels and other treasures were lost as the king and his party cross the Wash off the coast of Norfolk.

By the end of the month King John was dead at Newark Castle in Nottinghamshire. It is said he died of dysentery – a common enough disease in England at the time – aggravated by eating too many peaches and drinking 'too new' cider. John's nine-year old son Henry was left to rule over an English kingdom in debt and turmoil, and a greatly reduced Angevin inheritance.

HENRY III

1216–1272

Not only was Henry III just a boy when he succeeded to the throne, he inherited a kingdom that was in the middle of a civil war, with London and the south-east under the rule of Louis the Dauphin of France. And, because his father had lost most of the crown jewels in the North Sea while he was trying to cross the Wash, Henry had to be crowned king of England with his mother's bracelet at a makeshift ceremony in Gloucester Cathedral where the rest of the royal family had fled to safety. Fortunately, Henry had quite possibly the most respected man in England to act as his regent: William Marshal, Earl of Pembroke, was a brave and chivalrous knight who had served Henry II, Richard I and King John, and he vowed to carry the boy-king on his shoulders rather than allow him to fall to French rule. By the time Pembroke died in 1219, he had restored law and order to England: the rebel barons were defeated and Louis had been bribed to return home to France and, in 1217, renounced his claim to the throne of England.

The same year Henry signed a revised Magna Carta that helped to settle the unrest among the barons even further. In May 1220, Henry was crowned again, this time with new regalia and jewels at Westminster Abbey. But he was still only 12 years old and with no Pembroke to protect him or his interests, Henry became the pawn in the power struggles of Hubert de Burgh and Peter des Roches, Bishop of Winchester until Henry assumed direct rule in 1227. Although he was now king in his own right, Henry was perceived as weak and indecisive as a ruler: he lacked military prowess, preferred the arts to war, and appeared to favour foreigners over the English barons. Bishop Roches was from Poitou, a territory no longer held by the English and the barons became suspicious when he filled many important state posts with his fellow Poitevins. Following his marriage in 1236 to Eleanor of Provence, Henry alienated the English lords still further by allowing his wife's French relatives to swell the ranks of the English government.

Henry's court was indeed cosmopolitan and cultured, and the king saw to it that England's cultural life was expanded. He spent a great deal of time, money and love expanding the Tower of London (to include a menagerie), supervising the construction of St Alban's and Salisbury Cathedrals and the rebuilding of Westminster Abbey, including the gorgeous shrine to Edward the Confessor. Henry himself was fascinated by the cult of St Edward the Confessor, and made Westminster, where Edward had founded his abbey, the seat of his government. He endowed the first three colleges at the nascent University of Oxford, while in the monasteries, illuminated books and manuscripts were produced, notably under the leadership of the scholar-monk Matthew Paris, who was also a leading chronicler of the time.

HENRY III   1216–1272

Nicknames: *None known*
Dynasty: *House of Anjou/Plantagenet*
Born: *Winchester, Hampshire on
    1 October 1207*
Succeeded to Throne: *18 October 1216*
Crowned at: *Gloucester Cathedral on 28
    October 1216 and at
    Westminster Abbey on 17 May
    1220.*
Died: *Westminster Palace, London on
    16 November 1272*
Buried: *Westminster Abbey*

Authority: *King of England, with claims on
    Ireland, Scotland, Wales; Duke of
    Aquitaine.*
Parents: *King John and Isabella of Angouleme,
    their eldest son.*
Married: *Eleanor of Provence (died 1291),
    daughter of Count Raymond
    Berengaria IV of Provence on 20
    January 1276 at Canterbury.*
Children: *At least nine, notably Edward I*

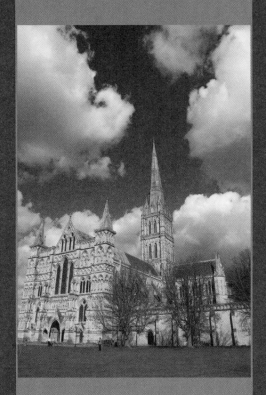

The main body of Salisbury Cathedral was completed in a remarkably quick 38 years, between 1220 and 1258, and is a fine example of Early English Gothic architecture.

At the Battle of Evesham, Simon de Montfort found himself on the defensive and was defeated by the royalist forces led by Prince Edward. The battle marked the end of baronial opposition to royal rule.

1216–1272

French Gothic art, architecture and literature became influential, especially the chansons and romans de gestes – the chivalric romances out of which would grow the stories of King Arthur and the knights of the Round Table – which came into their final form during Henry's reign.

Politically, an already tense situation was worsened by the imposition of heavy taxes (including the infamous scutage, a feudal tax imposed on knights in lieu of military service) defeats in Wales, a failed attempt in France to regain lost lands and Henry's efforts to make his son Edmund 'Crouchback' (in account of his deformity) king of Sicily by funding a campaign using monies raised for a crusade.

It was too much for the barons. In 1258 at the Council of Westminster opposition was led by the Marshal of England, Roger Bigod, Earl of Norfolk, and was followed by what became called the 'Mad Parliament' at Oxford where Henry was forced by his own brother-in-law, Simon de Montfort to acknowledge a new charter, the Provisions of Oxford, which allowed the barons to select half of the King's Council and thus attacked the king's absolute authority. In 1259, the Treaty of Paris confirmed Plantagenet losses: all of the former English possessions in France – Normandy, Anjou and Maine – were handed over to Louis IX of France. Only Gascony remained in English hands, but even this was to be held only as a fiefdom, subject to King Louis.

When Henry returned to England in 1260, with papal support, he denounced de Montfort and overturned the Provisions of Oxford. Once again England was thrown in conflict: in 1264 Henry was captured at the Battle of Lewes and de Montfort forced the king to submit to the barons' demands. Henry's son Prince Edward, who had escaped capture, formed an army and at the Battle of Evesham in 1265, triumphed over de Montfort who was killed (and his enemies took their revenge on his body by cutting off his hands, feet and genitals). After Evesham, Prince Edward took an increasingly active role in government, leaving his father free to pursue his patronage of the arts.

While he may not have been the strongest of monarchs, Henry's reign was the longest of any medieval king, at a remarkable 56 years. He may have lost the Angevin territories in France that his ancestors had fought so hard to gain and keep, but Henry III was responsible for the flowering of art and culture in England, and when he died peacefully at the Palace of Westminster in 1272, England was prosperous, cultured and, more importantly, united, and prepared to accept the rule of his son Edward without complaint.

EDWARD I

1272–1307

Nicknamed 'Longshanks' because of his 6ft (2m) height, Edward was 33 years old when he succeeded to the throne. He was born with a drooping eyelid, black hair that turned snowy white in his later years, and a fiery temper like many of his Plantagenet forebears. For a long time Edward was regarded as England's greatest king: a great soldier (he had fought at Acre during the Eighth Crusade in 1271), a pacifier and institutor of parliamentary and constitutional reforms. However, he could also be a bully, and was ambitious and devious. While he never succeeded in subduing the Scots – whose patriotic fervour for their leader Robert the Bruce was unparalleled – Edward earned the soubriquet 'Hammer of the Scots' for his dogged persistence and for stealing the Stone of Scone (or the 'Stone of Destiny' upon which the Scottish kings had been crowned and which was only returned to Scotland in 1996) to Westminster Abbey.

When his father died in 1272, Edward was on crusade. Unusually, he did not hurry home, partly because he had been injured, but also because he was confident that England was stable and well-governed. He finally arrived home in 1274 and was crowned in August.

In 1254, aged just 15, Edward had married Eleanor of Castile. She accompanied Edward on crusade in 1270–73 and gave birth to at least three of their 16 children while abroad. When she died in 1290, aged 54, Edward was heartbroken. As her body was taken from Lincoln to London, at each of the 12 places her funeral procession halted, Edward ordered the erection of monumental crosses that became known as 'Eleanor Crosses', some of which are still standing today, and one of which gave London's Charing Cross its name.

Between 1274 and 1290, Edward began a series of reforms to bring into check the corruption that the barons had enjoyed during the chaotic reigns of John and Henry. Edward was astute enough to realise that any new legislation or taxes would need the backing of the barons: commissioners were dispatched to survey the country, record local administration (known as the Hundred Rolls) and identify any legal abuses. From this, all rights claimed by barons now had to be clearly defined and had to be recorded. Furthermore, these rights needed to have existed prior to the reign of Richard I and were not based on the notion that the rights had been held since 'time immemorial'. By 1275, the Statute of Westminster had codified 51 laws (many of which came from the Magna Carta). In 1278 the writs of the Quo Warranto established ownership of lands, and the Statute of Winchester in 1285 dealt with the problems of highway robbery and violence by giving local residents the power to police their own communities, with newly appointed Justices of the Peace administering the law. By any standards, this was a considerable body of legislative reform, and although Edward did not claw back any power for the crown, he established the principle that all rights and privileges emanated from the king.

EDWARD I   1272–1307

Nicknames: *Longshanks ('Long Legs'); Hammer of the Scots (from the 16th century inscription on his tomb); the Lawgiver; the English Justinian.*

Dynasty: *House of Plantagenet*

Born: *Westminster Palace on 17 June 1239*

Succeeded to Throne: *20 November 1272*

Crowned at: *18 August 1274*

Died: *Burgh-by-Sands, near Carlisle on 7 July 1307*

Buried: *Westminster Abbey*

Authority: *King of England, Wales, Scotland and Ireland, the Isle of Man (from1290) and Duke of Aquitaine.*

Parents: *Henry III and Eleanor of Provence, their eldest surviving son.*

Married: *(1) Eleanor of Castile (c. 1244–90), daughter of King Ferdinand III of Castile on 25 October 1254 at Las Heuglas Monastery, Spain, and (2) Margaret of France (1282–1317), daughter of King Philip III of France, on 10 September 1299 at Canterbury, Kent.*

Children: *Sixteen by (1) notably Joan (1272–1307), Margaret (1275–1318), and Edward II; three by (2), notably Thomas of Brotherton (1300–38) and Edmund of Woodstock (died 1330).*

Edward's wars with the Scots have assumed something of a legendary status. When he was arrested and charged with treason, William Wallace declared. 'I could not be a traitor to Edward, for I was never his subject'.

The Eleanor Cross at Charing Cross, London is a replica of one of the 12 commemorative crosses erected in memory of Edward's queen, Eleanor of Castile.

1272–1307

By the end of Edward's reign, the 'Model Parliament' as it came to be known, had evolved to include representatives from the barons, the clergy, knights and burghers from the towns. Edward needed a compliant parliament in order to gather the taxes need to finance the wars which were a feature of the second half of his reign. The need to fill the royal coffers was also behind his persecution and expulsion of the Jews in 1290.

Incensed by the failure of the leading Welsh prince Llywelyn ap Gruffydd to do him homage, and tired of the border raids, in 1277 Edward marched on Wales, forcing Gruffydd to surrender. An uneasy peace held for five years, until with Welsh resentment of English rule growing, and Gruffydd again stirring up dissent, Edward invaded, this time intent on conquering the principality. In a series of campaigns, he subdued the Welsh, and like his Norman ancestors, built a series of monumental castles as a sign of English overlordship.

Relations with Scotland remained peaceful until the succession crisis caused by the death of Alexander III in 1286. Edward was asked to adjudicate, but insisted that the Scottish lords acknowledge him as overlord, which they refused to do. In 1296 the Scots allied with the French and attacked Carlisle. Edward retaliated and crushed Scottish resistance at the Battle of Dunbar, which he followed by snatching the ancient Stone of Scone. Scottish resentment of English actions simmered and boiled over when the Scots' leader, William Wallace, attacked the English and defeated them at the Battle of Stirling. Eight years of inconclusive fighting followed, until Wallace was captured and executed in 1305. When Robert the Bruce seized the Scottish throne in 1306 and launched another campaign for Scottish independence, Edward set off for the north, but the effort killed him. The 'Hammer of the Scots' became ill near Carlisle, where he died in 1307.

The king's body was brought south and was buried in Westminster Abbey. On his tomb are carved the words *pactum serva* ('Keep your word'). His administrative legacy was a great one: he reformed parliament, refined the legal system and generally improved the governance of England. His unfinished business with the Scots, however, left a troubled future ahead for his heir, Edward II.

EDWARD II

1307–1327

Like his father, Edward II was tall and good-looking; unlike his father he was interested in artistic pursuits rather than military campaigns and the rigours of government. The youngest child of Edward I and Eleanor of Castile, Edward was born in Carnaervon, where he was presented to the assembled (and probably recalcitrant) Welsh barons by his father, who said, 'Here is your Prince of Wales'. The title was officially ratified in 1301.

When he inherited the throne of England in 1307, the country was stable and prosperous, but Edward's reign would see it descend into chaos and near anarchy. His dying father's wish was that his son continued the campaigns against Robert the Bruce to bring Scotland under the control of the English crown. Edward made one attempt in Ayrshire but returned quickly to London to be in the company of his favourite courtiers. Chief among these were Piers Gaveston with whom Edward had a controversial and probably homosexual relationship. Gaveston was showered with riches and favours: he was given the earldom of Cornwall and was allowed to act as Edward's regent while he was abroad in France marrying Isabella, the daughter of Philip III of France. Outraged by Gaveston's behaviour, the barons banished him to Ireland only to see Edward bring him back within the year. In 1311, the barons, led by Thomas Lancaster, Edward's cousin, formed a council (the Lord's Ordainers) that forced Edward to banish Gaveston. When Edward again let his favourite return, in 1312 Gaveston was beheaded. Edward's grief at the loss of his friend was profound, and when it lessened he sought to punish those who had betrayed him.

Partly to divert the baron's attentions from his personal activities, in 1314 Edward went to the aid of the governor of Stirling Castle – one of the few English-held castles north of the border – which was under siege by Robert the Bruce. Edward's vast forces met the much smaller Scottish army at Bannockburn on 23 June in a two-day battle. In spite of the overwhelming military advantages, the battle was a disaster for Edward, and Scottish independence from England was firmly established.

After Gaveston's death, Edward promoted another favourite, Hugh Despenser the Younger. Despenser and his father (also Hugh) were corrupt, cruel and highly ambitious. Back in England, support for Edward began to dissolve and was split into pro-royalist factions led by the Despensers who had a power base in Wales, and anti-royalist factions led by Lancaster, who with a large private army was effectively in control of England. When Lancaster joined forces with Roger Mortimer to oust the Despensers, Edward finally acted. He led a campaign against Lancaster, captured and executed him in 1322, and took Mortimer prisoner.

EDWARD II   1307–1327

Nicknames: *Edward of Caernarvon*

Dynasty: *House of Plantagenet*

Born: *Caernarvon Castle, North Wales on 25 April 1284*

Succeeded to Throne: *7 July 1307*

Crowned at: *Westminster Abbey on 25 February 1308*

Died: *Berkeley Castle, Gloucestershire on 21 September 1327*

Buried: *Gloucester Cathedral*

Authority: *King of England and Wales, with claims on Ireland, Scotland, the Isle of Man (until 1313), Duke of Aquitaine*

Parents: *Edward I and Eleanor of Castile, their fourth son.*

Married: *Isabella (1292–1358) daughter of King Philip III of France on 25 January 1308 at Boulogne, France.*

Children: *Four, notably Edward III*

Edward II was buried in
Gloucester Cathedral.

Robert the Bruce defeated the English at
Bannockburn in 1314.

The royal favourites the Despensers were back at Edward's side, the Lords Ordainers were dissolved and any existing legislation that limited royal power was either revoked or simply ignored. In 1324, Mortimer escaped from the Tower of London and became the lover of Edward's wife, Isabella (who despite bearing the king four children was most likely concerned by her husband's sexual preferences), joining her in France. When Edward and Isabella's son Prince Edward went to visit his mother in France, Isabella refused to allow him to return to England: she and Mortimer planned to overthrow Edward and place the young prince on the throne. Successfully raising a mercenary army, Isabella and Mortimer's forces landed in England in September 1326 and in January 1327, Edward was forced to abdicate the throne in favour of his 14-year-old son.

Edward was imprisoned, first at Kenilworth, and then in Berkeley Castle in Gloucestershire where it is believed that Edward was murdered in the most horrible manner on the orders of Mortimer. In order to make his death 'look natural', Mortimer had to ensure that Edward's body would not bear any outwardly visible marks of violence: starvation took too long so Edward's death was to be by disembowelment, the conventional method of execution for homosexuals at this time: *cum vero ignitio inter celanda confossus*, a red hot poker was inserted into his rectum up into his bowels. Some historians do, however, believe that he escaped and lived the rest of his life in exile

Sadly for his reputation, Edward II is a king wedged between two very effective monarchs – his father and his son. He inherited a problematic situation in Scotland from his father, but he seems to have been temperamentally unsuited to the duties of kingship. His military leadership was disasterous and his habit of promoting ambitious and greedy favourites discredited his government. It is clear from the events surrounding Isabella and Mortimer's invasion in 1326 that Edward was monumentally unpopular: few of the barons hesitated or wavered before joining forces with the Queen's coup, and even the king's close relatives, such as his half-brother and own son abandoned him.

EDWARD III

1327–1377

Only 14 years old when he succeeded to the throne, Edward III's role as monarch was overseen by his mother Queen Isabella, who acted as regent with her lover Roger Mortimer until 1330. In 1330 Edward launched a coup by summoning a parliament at Nottingham. Edward sneaked into the castle at night with a few supporters and captured Roger Mortimer from his mother's bed, convicted him under an Act of Attainder as an enemy of the state and had him executed at Tyburn. Isabella was 'retired' from public life and spent the rest of her life confined at Castle Rising in Norfolk.

Edward III's 50-year reign was marked by key events at home and abroad: first, his ambitions for ruling Scotland were re-kindled. Robert the Bruce had been replaced by the boy-king David II and Edward backed Edward Balliol's claim to Scotland. David was overthrown in 1332 but Balliol's hold was tenuous. In July 1333, Edward effectively ended the Scottish Wars of Independence by inflicting a crushing defeat on the Scots at Halidon Hill near Berwick-upon-Tweed and Balliol managed to maintain his grip over Scotland— at least until 1336 when he was deposed for the final time with David II restored to the throne.

The second major event was the Hundred Years War with France (which started in 1337 and went on sporadically for some 115 years until 1453). It is said it dragged on for so long because at the beginning Philip VI of France refused to fight – even when Edward offered him the chivalrous opportunity to settle the matter in one-to-one knightly combat. Edward claimed the French throne through his mother Isabella but the Hundred Years War was not only about claims to lands in France, as Edward, through his marriage to Philippa of Hainault (to whom he was devoted) wanted to expand and consolidate the valuable wool trade with Flanders. In a significant naval battle, Edward's fleet destroyed the French fleet off Sluys in 1340, then in 1346 used the English archers with their longbows to win the Battle of Crecy. The next year, Edward's tactic was to starve Calais into surrender: the city held out for a long time and it was down to Queen Philippa's intercession that Edward did not hang the capitulating burghers of Calais who had held out against him for so long.

For the next ten years, Edward's son, Edward, Prince of Wales – the Black Prince – raided south-west France. He captured the king, Jean II and paved the way for the Treaty of Bretigny in 1360, when Edward renounced his claim on the French throne in exchange for rule over Calais, Poitou and Aquitaine with the Black Prince ruling Bordeaux. War resumed eight years later, and this time Edward's gains became losses – largely due to the destructiveness of his sons. Edward III was the first monarch to grant dukedoms of English territories: while he and his forebears had adopted titles such as Duke of Normandy or Aquitaine, Edward made his heir Duke of Cornwall

EDWARD III   1327–1377

Nicknames: Edward of Windsor, 'King of the Sea'.

Dynasty: House of Plantagenet

Born: Windsor Castle, Berkshire on 13 November 1312

Succeeded to Throne: 25 January 1327

Crowned at: Westminster Abbey on 29 January 1327

Died: Sheen Palace, Surrey on 21 June 1377

Buried: Westminster Abbey

Authority: King of England and Wales, with claims over Ireland, Scotland and the Isle of Man (from 1333) and France (from 1340).

Parents: Edward II and Isabella of France, their elder son.

Married: Philippa of Hainault (c.1314–69), daughter of Count William I of Hainault and Holland on 24 January 1328 at York.

Children: Twelve, notably Edward the Black Prince (1330–76), Lionel of Antwerp (1338–68), John of Gaunt (1340–99), Thomas of Woodstock (1355–97) and Edmund of Langley (1341–1402).

The English defeated a larger French force at Crecy in 1346 thanks, in part, to the firepower of the English archers.

Plague killed nearly half the population.

Edward the Black Prince died in 1376, a year before his father.

1327–1377

(as well as Prince of Wales); Lionel was Duke of Antwerp as well as the Duke of Clarence and earl of Ulster; John of Gaunt (named after his birthplace) was titled Duke of Lancaster; Edward of Langley was Duke of York, and, Thomas of Woodstock was Duke of Gloucester. By the time Edward III died, there was little to show for the English conquest in France beyond the fortresses at Calais, Bordeaux and Bayonne.

The third major event of Edward's reign came in 1349 when the Black Death spread across Europe. It is difficult to underestimate the upheaval this caused: chroniclers reported that there were barely enough people left to bury the dead. The economic consequences were tremendous: with up to 40 percent of the population dead, the survivors struggled for survival – no one was left to work the fields and with the shortage of labour and food, prices increased dramatically. In England, one immediate effect was a suspension of the fighting in France. Labourers left alive began to demand higher wages and in 1351 Edward's government passed the Statute of Labourers, which fixed wages at pre-plague levels.

Edward's contribution to legal and parliamentary reforms are often overlooked, but he was fortunate to have the support of a number of competent and trustworthy advisors, such as William de Wykeham, William Montacute and William de Bohun. Parliament evolved during his reign into a bicameral institution, with the houses of lords and commons becoming separate entities. In 1351 the Statute of Treason laid down the definition of high treason, while other laws made it illegal to raise any taxes without the consent of parliament.

It had popularly been called the age of chivalry, and Edward III played a full part. He rebuilt Windsor Castle and in 1348 founded the Order of the Garter. English, rather than Norman-French became not only the official language used in parliament and the law courts, but gave rise to a flowering of English literature: Geoffrey Chaucer (who was a page to Edward's son Lionel, Duke of Clarence) wrote his most famous work *The Canterbury Tales* between 1387–98.

When Queen Philippa died in 1369, Edward consoled himself with the company of several mistresses, notably Alice Perrers. In the summer of 1377 at Sheen, plagued by shingles and heart problems, Edward suffered a terminal stroke. Mistress Alice regarded the paralysed king, stripped the jewels from his fingers and fled the scene. Found by a priest, Edward is said to have muttered his final words *Miserere Jesu* before he died.

Edward III is regarded as a successful English king. He was victorious in battle and his regime survived one of the greatest natural disasters of the last millennium, the Black Death. Unlike many of his predecessors, he was blessed with loyal sons, who upheld the succession of their nephew.

RICHARD II

1377–1399

The son of the Edward 'the Black Prince', Richard II was born in Bordeaux in France where his father was ruler. His father died in 1376 and Richard became Prince of Wales and Duke of Cornwall. The following year, on the death of his grandfather Edward III, Richard became king aged ten. A regency council governed the country until 1380.

The kingdom Richard inherited was exhausted by war, financially drained by the heavy taxation that paid for the campaigns, and with a population unsettled by the economic and social effects of the Black Death. In 1381, popular discontent boiled over. Tensions between landowners and peasants were exacerbated by the imposition of the Poll Tax, which was just one tax too many for a population already struggling with inflated prices. They deplored the imbalance of wealth in the kingdom and the clergy's economic and political power. In addition, Richard's regents – particularly his uncle John of Gaunt and the Lord Treasurer Sir Robert Hales – were unpopular and were thought to be exploiting the king's youth and weakness.

The rebellion broke out in Kent and Essex in May 1381 and the rebels marched on London. Responding with great courage and initiative, Richard met with Watt Tyler and John Ball, two of the leaders, promising to meet some of their demands. In the ensuing dispute, Tyler was killed by one of the king's party. Richard managed to reconcile the rebels, but later rescinded the pardons he had granted the rebels and hanged the leader. Consequently, Richard's name and character became blackened. Richard had seen with his own eyes the dangers of opposition to royal authority, and this may have shaped his later despotic attitudes to ruling.

Unlike his father and uncles, Richard had no real interest in warfare: for most of his reign he was forced to deal with the power struggles of his three ambitious uncles, the Dukes of York, Lancaster and Gloucester. John of Gaunt, Duke of Lancaster, had his eye on the throne, an ambition he passed on to his son Henry of Bolingbroke, Earl of Derby. Richard attempted to counter this by ruling autocratically: by the time he was 19 he had pretty much replaced the power of parliament and was ruling through appointments he had made to court favourites. Unfortunately, the number of people in Richard's 'household' soon numbered some 10,000 people– a huge burden on England's finances.

The war with France dragged on, and in 1385, with a real threat of a French invasion, Gaunt urged the launch of an expedition to protect English possessions. Instead, encouraged by his chancellor Michael

RICHARD II   1377–1399

Nicknames: *Richard of Bordeaux*
Dynasty: *House of Plantagenet*
Born: *Bordeaux, France, on 6 January 1367*
Succeeded to Throne: *22 June 1377*
Crowned at: *Westminster Abbey on
    16 July 1367*
Died: *Pontefract Castle, Yorkshire on
    14 February 1400*
Buried: *Kings Langley, Hertfordshire, reburied
    at Westminster Abbey in 1413.*
Authority: *King of England and Wales with
    claims over Ireland and France.*

Parents: *Edward the Black Prince and Joan Of
    Kent, their second, only surviving son.*
Married: *(1) Anne of Bohemia (1366–94)
    daughter of Emperor Charles IV on
    20 January 1382 at St. Stephen's
    Chapel, Westminster;
    (2) Isabella (1389–1409) daughter
    of King Charles VI of France on 4
    November 1396 at St. Nicholas's
    Chapel, Westminster.*
Children: *None*

After his deposition in 1399, Richard II was imprisoned in Pontefract Castle.

The chronicler Jean Froissart was attached to the royal household from c. 1360. He travelled extensively and his Chronicles are the best source for the 14th century.

Wat Tyler led the Peasants' Revolt in 1381.

1377-1399

de la Pole Richard led an army against Scotland. When de la Pole requested unprecedented taxes from parliament in 1386, and further enraged by the appointment of Robert de Vere as Regent of Ireland, opposition to Richard's rule erupted.

Parliament demanded de la Pole's removal from office, threatening to depose the king if he did not give in. Richard set off on a journey around England to garner support and on his return in 1387 was met by the Lords Appellant – a council of nobles led by the earls of Derby (Henry Bolingbroke), Warwick, Arundel and Nottingham. They presided over the 'Merciless Parliament' of 1388, effectively seizing control of England and forcing some of Richard's officials into exile.

A year later Richard reached majority age and staged a coup resuming his 'personal' government. In 1382, Richard had married Anne of Bohemia, in a royal and political alliance that lasted 12 years and grew into devotion to each other, despite the fact they had no children. When Anne died in 1394, Richard lost the one modifying influence on his character and reign: he became more autocratic – tending towards absolutism – and his 'aestheticism' (some might say 'dandyism') became more exaggerated, extravagant and expensive. Richard was a patron of the poets John Gower and Geoffrey Chaucer, as well as the chronicler John Froissart, and it is said, introduced the fashion for handkerchiefs. The same year 1394, Richard launched a semi-successful campaign to subdue Ireland – he would be the only reigning monarch to set foot in Ireland between 1210 and the late 17th century – and negotiated a truce with France, sealing the alliance by marrying Isabella, the seven-year-old daughter of King Charles VI of France.

Richard had neither forgotten nor forgiven the humiliating events of 1387, and in 1397, the five dissident Lords Appellants were arrested, executed or exiled and their estates forfeited and divided among Richard's favourites. Bolingbroke was banished from England for ten years – and this was extended to life after his father John of Gaunt died. Free from restraint, Richard seemed to descend into despotism and the barons became alarmed.

When Richard left for a second campaign in Ireland, Bolingbroke returned to England with a small army and found most allegiance to the king had vanished. Bolingbroke saw his chance to seize power. By August 1399, Richard had been captured and imprisoned in the Tower of London. In September, Richard II, who was without a son and heir, abdicated, and was moved to Pontefract castle where he died, apparently of starvation.

HOUSE OF
LANCASTER
1399–1461

The House of Lancaster was a branch of the House of Anjou (or Plantagenet) and was a short-lived dynasty of just three monarchs, all of whom were named Henry. The period of their rule in England was marked by warfare: there was revolt among the barons, rebellion in Wales, prolonged war with France when the Hundred Years War reopened in 1415, and, the dynastic Wars of the Roses between 1455–85.

The political situation was exacerbated by the after-effects of the Black Death that killed nearly half of the English population: lawlessness was rife and without sufficient peasants to cultivate the land, the cost of labour escalated as did the price of food. The first Lancastrian king, Henry IV would constantly be hindered by a lack of money.

OWAIN GLYN DWR, OR GLENDOWER, PRINCE OF WALES

Owain Glyn Dwr was the last Welsh national to claim the title 'Prince of Wales'. Descended from Madog ap Maredudd (the last ruler of a united Powys) and Rhys ap Gruffyd, Lord of Deheubarth, Owain was born sometime around 1354 and around 1383 married Margaret, the daughter of David Hanmer, a Justice of the King's Bench. It appears that Owain had both a legal and a military training and he became the voice of Welshmen discontented over their treatment by their English overlords.

A border dispute enflamed tempers and in September 1400, Owain's supporters declared him Prince of Wales. After Henry IV sent English troops to Wales, Owain went into hiding, but during the next four years maintained a guerrilla war: in April 1401 the Welsh seized Conway Castle and the next English expedition succeeded in bringing greater support to the Welsh from Scotland and Ireland. In 1402 Owain's forces overwhelmed the English at Bryn Glas and captured the leader of the English 'Lords of the Marches', Edmund Mortimer.

Mortimer was eventually won over to the Welsh cause and married Owain's daughter Katherine and soon other factions from England and France – including Henry 'Hotspur' Percy, Earl of Northumberland – came to the aid of the Welsh. By 1405, however, Owain's alliance with Northumberland and Mortimer began to unravel: it appeared that they were plotting the overthrow of Henry IV and planning to divide England (and Wales) between themselves. Although their plans came to naught, Owain's fortunes, along with those of Mortimer and Percy, began to wane. Northumberland's forces suffered a defeat and the promised support from Scotland and France never materialized. When Northumberland died in 1408, Owain's support in England vanished and soon the English regained the Welsh castles. The final two Welsh strongholds, the castles at

1399–1461

Aberystwyth and Harlech, where Mortimer died and Owain's wife and many of their children were captured, fell in 1409. Owain was once again forced into hiding along with his son Maredudd. He was never betrayed but the rebellion was over and Wales was subdued. Owain was presumed dead in 1415–16, his final resting place unknown.

THE HUNDRED YEARS WAR: SUCCESSES AND LOSSES

The long war with France that began with Edward III's claim to the French throne in 1337 was fought sporadically until 1453. The third and final phase of the war began with Henry V's success at Agincourt in 1415. The English troops were already tired from their siege of the naval port of Harfleur and were further weakened by dysentery. As winter approached, Henry decided to make his way to the English stronghold at Calais. In the meantime, Charles d'Albret, Constable of France was amassing a vast feudal army some 20,000 strong and it was this army that confronted the depleted English army that now numbered a mere 6,000 on 25 October 1415. The odds of an English victory were overwhelming, but the muddy field of battle favoured the lightly armoured English troops who had the 'advanced technology' of the longbow. French losses have been estimated as high as 7,000; English losses at around 500. While the victory at Agincourt gained Henry little in terms of territory, the overwhelming win against French nobles and their forces made success in subsequent campaigns more likely. Furthermore, it won Henry the support of the Holy Roman Emperor and made him a hero in England.

In 1417 Henry was back campaigning in France; in 1419, Normandy was back under English control, and Henry was at the walls of Paris. By the Treaty of Troyes of May 1420, Henry V would become king of France on the death of Charles VI and marry the king's daughter Catherine of Valois. With support from the Burgundian faction, Henry agreed to resume his war against the Dauphin (the pretender to the French throne). It looked as though Henry would be triumphant but his last victory came in May 1422 at Meaux, the Dauphin's stronghold and by August, weakened by dysentery, Henry V died outside Paris before he could become king. The English victories in France were not to last: Henry's son and heir Henry VI was just a year old when he inherited the two thrones of England and France and his rule abroad was to be undermined by a simple, peasant girl.

JOAN OF ARC: THE MAID OF ORLEANS

Born in Domremy in eastern France, Joan of Arc was a peasant girl who in 1429 claimed to have had a vision in which she was told to drive the English out of France. At Chinon in north-west France she managed to persuade the Dauphin of her divine mission. Fierce fighting between the forces of the Dauphin, and Henry VI's regent, his uncle John, Duke of Bedford, centred around the city of Orleans, which had been under constant siege since 1427. Although she was only 17, Joan

Sculpture of Owain Glyndwr.

Agincourt – a might victory for Henry V.

Joan of Arc, who inspired the French and was burnt at the stake in Rouen by the English.

The Yorkist Edward IV secured his claim to the throne at the Battle of Barnet in 1471.

led an army and raised the siege in May 1429. Further victory followed at Patay (north of Orleans) that lifted the spirits of the French. In June 1429, the Dauphin was crowned as Charles VII of France at Rheims. The Maid of Orleans, however, failed to take Paris that was held by the Burgundian allies of the English, and in May 1430 she was captured and 'sold' to the English. A tribunal of French ecclesiastics supported by the English found Joan guilty of witchcraft and heresy, and on 30 May 1431 in Rouen she was burned at the stake. Joan had started a campaign that would see the English expelled from all of its French lands except Calais by 1453.

DYNASTIC QUARRELS: THE WARS OF THE ROSES

On-going family disputes between two branches of the ruling Plantagenets, the houses of York and Lancaster eventually descended into conflict in the Wars of the Roses between 1455 and 1485. This was not true 'civil war' as not all the classes of English society were involved: on the contrary, agricultural output grew, merchants were unaffected and domestic and international trade boomed. The Wars of the Roses take their name from the emblems used by each house: the Lancastrians sported a red rose, the Yorkists, a white rose. The quarrel between Lancaster and York had its roots in 1399 when Henry, Duke of Lancaster, son of John of Gaunt, deposed Richard II. John of Gaunt was Edward III's third son, while the rival Yorkists were descended from Edward's second and fourth sons, thereby giving them a rival claim on the English throne.

The three Lancastrian kings reigned from 1399–1461, and the Yorkists from 1461–1485, with a brief interruption in 1470–71, when the Yorkist Edward IV was deposed in favour of the Lancastrian Henry VI. The situation was further complicated after 1422, when the infant Henry VI succeeded to the throne. His minority enabled a number of nobles to manoeuvre for power, and circumstances did not change much once he reached his majority.

In the 30 years' fighting from the first Battle at St Albans in 1455, to the decisive Battle of Bosworth in 1485, there were just ten major battles. The warfare was not constant, and actual 'engagement' averaged just one week every two-and-half years, with the armies on each side composed largely of noblemen, their sons and retainers along with foreign mercenary soldiers. It would not be until 1485 that peace was restored, when the first Tudor monarch, the Lancastrian Henry VII defeated Richard III and brought the wars to an end. His marriage to Elizabeth of York, the daughter of Edward IV united the two warring 'roses', which were now combined into the Tudor Rose.

HENRY IV

1399–1413

Son of John of Gaunt, Duke of Lancaster, Henry IV was intelligent and literate (he corresponded with many heads of state including the emperors of Byzantium and Abyssinia and even with the Mongol leader, Tamerlain); an accomplished musician and sponsor of poets (he increased Chaucer's pension); pious (he made pilgrimage to Jerusalem); an excellent swordsman (he had fought with the Teutonic Knights in Lithuania) and an extremely astute and ambitious politician.

A grandson of Edward III, Henry Bolingbroke came to rule England by seizing the crown from his cousin Richard II. Henry took advantage of the restlessness of the barons against Richard and eventually forced him to abdicate. Richard was imprisoned and starved to death and his corpse publicly displayed – to show there were no visible marks or injuries – so he would no longer be the focus of dissent. Richard's designated heir was, in fact, Edmund, 5th Earl of March, a great-grandson of Lionel, Duke of Clarence, Edward III's second son. Fully aware of the fact that young Edmund was descended from a senior branch of the family, Henry imprisoned him in Windsor for the entire length of his reign.

Although he had the backing of some powerful magnates, Henry had to work hard to consolidate his rule: in exchange for support – and money – from parliament. He had to concede the right of the Commons to freedom of speech, while the church insisted that he carried out the 'witch-hunts' that Richard had resisted. During Henry's reign the first 'heretics' were burnt at the stake. Many of the lords also wanted power and wealth and Henry allowed them to campaign in France, Wales and against the Scots. In sanctioning these actions, Henry opened the doors to the barons eventually revolting against him: the Earl of Worcester, the Earl of Northumberland and his son 'Harry Hotspur', as well as Archbishop Richard le Scrope of York were all in open rebellion, which Henry ended at the Battle of Shrewsbury (1403). His execution of the popular archbishop in 1405 made him unpopular, but together, these events crushed the opposition to him.

When the Welsh rebellions led by Owain Glyn Dwr ended in 1409 Henry's rule seemed secure: rebels in England and Wales had been subdued, James I of Scotland, whom Henry had captured in 1407, was a prisoner in England, and France, despite not recognising Henry as king, was too involved in its own disputes about the royal succession to be a threat to England. Henry, though, was always extremely anxious about his 'usurpation' of the throne and seemed prematurely aged and plagued by a guilty conscience. His last five years were spent in ill health and in the shadow of his more popular son, Henry of Monmouth, the future Henry V, who had set up his own court to challenge his father's. Henry died of heart disease, but at the same time was hugely troubled by a disfiguring skin condition that many – and possibly he too – believed was divine retribution for the overthrow and murder of Richard II.

HENRY IV

Nicknames: *Henry of Bolingbroke*
Dynasty: *House of Lancaster*
Born: *Bolingbroke Castle,*
Lincolnshire in April 1366
Succeeded to Throne: *30 September*
1399
Crowned at: *Westminster Abbey on*
13 October 1399
Died: *Jerusalem Chamber, Westminster Palace*
on 20 March 1413
Buried: *Canterbury Cathedral, Kent*
Authority: *King of England and Wales, with*
claims over France and Ireland

Parents: *John of Gaunt and Blanche of*
Lancaster, their eldest son.
Married: *(1) Mary de Bohun (1368/70–94),*
daughter of Humphrey X, Earl of
Hereford in 1380/81 at Rochford
in Essex; (2) Joan of Navarre
(c.1370–1437), daughter of King
Charles II of Navarre on 7 February
1403 at Winchester, Hampshire.
Children: *Seven by (1) notably Henry V*

HENRY V   1413–1422

Nicknames: Henry of Monmouth

Dynasty: House of Lancaster

Born: Monmouth on 9 August or
16 September 1387

Succeeded to Throne: 20 March 1413

Crowned at: Westminster Abbey
on 9 April 1413

Died: Vincennes castle, near Paris on
31 August 1422

Buried: Chapel of the Confessor,
Westminster Abbey

Authority: King of England and Wales, ruling
parts of Ireland and France (was
Regent in 1420), and Duke of
Normandy from 1417.

Parents: Henry IV and Mary de Bohun, their
second and surviving son.

Married: Catherine of Valois (1401–37),
youngest daughter of King Charles
VI of France on 2 June 1420 at St.
John's Church, Troyes, France.

Children: Henry VI

1413-1422

As a boy Henry of Monmouth had been treated kindly by Richard II, in spite of his father's behaviour: when Henry Bolingbroke seized the throne he swore that what he had 'gained by the sword' would be 'kept by his son's sword'. The last of the great warrior-kings of the Middle Ages, Henry succeeded to the throne aged 25. Apart from one act of rebellion by Edmund, Earl of March whom Henry had released from imprisonment, there was little serious opposition to his rule. To divert the baron's attention away from any further thoughts of rebellion, his first real act as king was to re-open the Hundred Years War with France to win back English territories lost by his ancestors. Reviving his ancestor Edward III's claim to the throne of France, Henry sailed for France in mid-1415 to lay siege to Harfleur. When the town fell, he challenged the Dauphin of France to personal combat with the prize to the victor being Normandy, Anjou, Maine and Touraine, and Henry's marriage to the Dauphin's sister, Catherine. The Dauphin ignored the offer and Henry marched to Calais and met, and defeated a huge French army in a muddy field at Agincourt in October 1415.

Since nearly the entire male nobility of England were with Henry at this time, the success served to strengthen Henry's position as king. A two-year break in the war then saw Henry back in England before he returned to France in 1417 and conquered Normandy. His reputation for being merciful to his enemies was tarnished when he refused the safe passage of non-combatants through the

English lines of those expelled from the besieged town of Rouen. During the six-month siege, Henry watched as some 12,000 civilians starved to death in the ditches outside the town walls. After further military successes, in 1420 he negotiated the Treaty of Troyes, which recognised him as the next king of France instead of the Dauphin and gave him the hand of the king's daughter, Catherine whom he married in Paris. After a short trip to England to crown his queen, Henry returned to France to resume battle with the Dauphin. Success looked likely, but before Henry could succeed to the throne of France, he was struck down with dysentery in September 1422. Charles VI, the French king died the following month, which left Henry's 10- month-old son Henry VI as king of both countries.

HENRY VI

1422–61 & 1470–71

Henry VI was just ten months old when he became the king of England and the king of France. On his father's deathbed in Paris, provision had been made for a regency: the late king's brother, the Duke of Gloucester was named Protector of England and another brother, the Duke of Bedford, was named Regent of France. At the same time, the Dauphin of France – Charles VI's son who had been 'passed over' by the Treaty of Troyes – was also declared king of France so Anglo-French hostilities were to continue. The vast territories won by the English under Henry V seemed secure: the Dauphin's troops were exhausted, and fighting had ended in stalemate. Suddenly, French resolve and fortune turned and it came in a form that took everyone by surprise: Joan of Arc, the 'Maid of Orleans', a young peasant girl who claimed visions from God had commanded her to raise and lead an army to victory against the English at the besieged city of Orleans in 1429. After a succession of victories, the Dauphin was crowned Charles VII of France at Rheims in June. In response the infant Henry VI was taken to Paris and crowned king of France (as Henri II).

Although Henry was the only king to be formally crowned in both kingdoms, the act did not rally the French to his side: in 1435 England's former allies the Burgundians withdrew their support and went over to Charles VII, and in 1436, Paris fell to his forces. Meanwhile, in England, the enormous cost of financing the war annoyed the barons and parliament, and Gloucester was proving a highly unpopular protector.

When Henry finally reached majority things were no better since he had little interest in government and gave authority and power to a few of his favourites, in particular, the Earl of Suffolk. Suffolk negotiated a five-year truce with France under the terms of which Henry would marry Charles's niece Margaret of Anjou (in April 1445) and the territory of Maine would be returned to France – a condition that was kept secret from parliament until Margaret and Suffolk convinced Henry to honour the terms of the treaty in 1447. Not surprisingly, this caused outrage among the English, and nor did it impress the French. A crisis was developing and Henry began to fear for his life. Suffolk and Margaret convinced Henry that Gloucester was plotting against him, so Henry had him arrested: he died a week later. Suffolk then decided to invade Brittany, a foolish action that led to the loss of the hard-won Normandy in 1450. For this, Suffolk was impeached, executed and posthumously blamed for everything that was wrong in Henry's kingdom.

Henry's choice of replacement for Suffolk was his new favourite, Edmund Beaufort, Earl of Somerset who now found himself blamed for the English losses at Rouen and after: Gascony (held for more than 300 years) fell in 1453 and Calais was left as the sole English possession. In less than 20 years,

HENRY VI   1422–1461
& 1470–1471

(Deposed 4 March 1461; restored 3 October 1470, and deposed 11 April 1471)

Nicknames: *None known*

Dynasty: *House of Lancaster*

Born: *Windsor Castle, Berkshire on 6 December 1421*

Succeeded to Throne: *1 September 1422*

Crowned at: *Westminster Abbey on 6 November 1429; St. Denis, Paris on 16 December 1431, and, St. Paul's Cathedral, London on 13 October 1470*

Died: *Tower of London, 21 May 1471*

Buried: *Chertsey Abbey, reburied in St. George's Chapel, Windsor castle in 1484*

Authority: *King of England and Wales, with control of parts of France (until 1453) and Ireland*

Parents: *Henry V and Catherine of Valois, their only child*

Married: *Margaret of Anjou (1430–82), daughter of Rene, Duc d'Anjou on 23 April 1445 at Tichfield Abbey, in the New Forest near Southampton.*

Children: *Edward, Prince of Wales (1453–71)*

Joan of Arc rallied the French and led them to victory against the English.

1422–1461 & 1470–1471

all the gains made by Henry V had been lost. To make matters worse, Henry now began to suffer his first bout of insanity. In March 1454 the Duke of York, a man hated by Somerset, was made Protector of the Realm. The enmity between Somerset and the Duke of York soon escalated into the war in 1461 Henry lost his crown to York's son Edward, whose position had been engineered by the Yorkist 'kingmaker' the Earl of Warwick. In October 1470, however, Edward and Warwick fell out and Henry was re-instated on the throne, a reign that would last only until April 1471: Edward returned with an army, defeated Warwick at Barnet (14 April) and took Henry prisoner. His only child, Edward, Prince of Wales was slain at the Battle of Tewkesbury (4 May) where Margaret was also captured: she was ransomed to the French in 1476 and returned to Anjou where she died in 1482. In May 1471, on the day Edward re-entered London, Henry VI was murdered in the Tower of London.

A pawn in the Yorkist and Lancastrian power games, Henry VI 's only real legacy, was his patronage of the arts. He founded both Eton College and King's College, Cambridge.

The Battle of Tewkesbury ended Lancastrian hopes of retaining the throne.

95

THE HOUSE OF YORK 1461–1485

Like the House of Lancaster, the House of York was a branch of the Plantagenet dynasty. The House of York was descended from two of Edward III's sons: Lionel, Duke of Clarence and Edmund, Duke of York. Lionel was the older brother of John of Gaunt who began the Lancastrian 'line' and consequently, the Yorkist monarchs had the more senior claim to the English throne. The Yorkist dynasty was founded by Richard Plantagenet, Duke of York, who challenged the rule of the Lancastrian king Henry VI and sparked the Wars of the Roses between the rival Plantagenets. Richard did not live to see the Yorks rule England. He was killed at the Battle of Wakefield in 1460 and it was his son, Edward IV that eventually deposed the insane Henry VI and seized the throne for himself and his heirs. York rule was not long – just 24 years – and saw only three kings succeed to the throne, only two of whom were actually crowned.

ART AND TRADE
In spite of sporadic conflict, when the inter-dynastic feuding of the Wars of the Roses continued until 1485, during the rule of the House of York there was a flowering of the arts and trade in England. With the end of the Hundred Years War with France, much of the money that had once been required to finance the military campaign was free for spending in other pursuits. In 1474 the Hanseatic League, a powerful confederation of northern European trading cities with a monopoly of the Baltic trade, was granted privileges to trade with England. The domestic wool and cloth trade also grew in this period and the value of the city guilds and livery companies (merchant companies) was recognised by the sovereign, who allowed them to directly elect the Lord Mayor of London. Edward also financed large-scale building works at Windsor Castle and Eltham Place in Kent.

CAXTON'S PRESS
Edward IV was a great patron of the arts and a pioneer patron of the new technology of the printing press: in 1476 Edward encouraged William Caxton to establish his printing press of moveable type at Westminster, and also helped to finance the first book printed in England, *The Dictes and Sayinges of the Phylosophers* which had been translated by the queen's brother, Anthony, Lord Rivers.

THE COLLEGE OF ARMS
Richard III founded the College of Arms: heralds were originally royal messengers but had developed into ten different types of courtier, who now also arranged coronations, weddings and funerals and read out royal proclamations among other tasks. With the huge rise in the number of 'noble families' all adopting coats of arms to identify them (since the overwhelming majority of the country were illiterate they relied on visual devices to recognise who was who), the heralds were called upon to regulate the design and award of coats of arms. In 1483 Richard III ordered the different heralds to be incorporated into the single 'college' which continues to control the issue of coats of arms today.

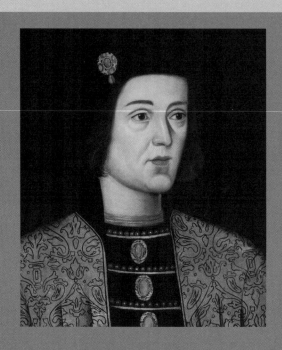

EDWARD IV
1461-1470 & 1471-1483

Nicknames: None known

Dynasty: House of York

Born: Rouen, France on 28 April 1442

Succeeded to Throne: (1) 4 March 1461 & (2) 11 April 1471

Crowned at: Westminster Abbey on 28 June 1461

Died: Westminster Palace on 9 April 1483

Buried: St. George's Chapel, Windsor Castle, Berkshire

Authority: King of England and Wales, ruling Calais and parts of Ireland

Parents: Richard, 3rd Duke of York, and Cicely, daughter of Ralph Neville, 1st Earl of Westmorland, their eldest son.

Married: Elizabeth Woodville (c.1437–92), daughter of Sir Richard Neville on 1 May 1464 at Grafton, Northants.

Children: Ten, notably Elizabeth, Edward V and Richard

1461–1470 & 1471–1483

At just 19 years old, Edward defeated the Lancastrian king Henry VI in battle at Mortimer's Cross and seized the crown. Edward was a good soldier and a competent ruler. England's finances had been depleted during the reign of Henry VI and Edward, living up to his motto of 'method and order' (*modus et ordo*), restored the financial machinery of government. At the start of his first reign Edward allowed his cousin, Richard Neville, the 'kingmaker' Earl of Warwick to govern the kingdom and defeat any remaining outposts of Lancastrian resistance to his rule, leaving Edward free to enrich the country's commercial activities in order to reduce the debts of the Crown.

Edward had a great interest in increasing trade by developing the English wool trade (under Edward cloth exports rose to their highest levels and overall trade doubled during his rule) and was a patron of William Caxton, who established his printing press at Westminster and produced the first books printed with moveable type in England.

Tall at 6 ft 4 in., handsome, and a fine dancer, Edward was also a glutton and apparently fond of rather dissolute sexual practices. In 1464, much to the annoyance of Warwick who as Chamberlain of England was the second most powerful man in England, Edward secretly married Elizabeth Woodville, the daughter of a knight but the widow of a commoner. Warwick had been working to secure an alliance with France that was supposed to be sealed with Edward's marriage to Bona of Savoy. Edward, however, had favoured an alliance with old allies the Burgundians (who were fighting against Louis). The story goes that Edward lusted after Elizabeth, who refused the king's advances without a promise of marriage. Under the pretext of a hunting trip, he travelled to Grafton Regis in Northamptonshire and married her. To make matters worse, Elizabeth already had two sons and the family were Lancastrian sympathisers. Their enemies also alleged that the marriage was bigamous, as Edward, who was already known for his philandering, appears to have made a similar 'marriage' promise to Lady Eleanor Butler a year or two earlier. Edward's sexual activities, which may have been exaggerated, would nonetheless, later be used by his enemies to challenge the legitimacy of his ten children.

Warwick was humiliated in the face of the French king and angry at Edward's continued preferences of Burgundian allies: the final insult was when Edward married off his sister Margaret to Charles, Duke of Burgundy in 1468. Warwick withdrew his support from the king and sided with Edward's ambitious brother George, Duke of Clarence who had his eye on the throne. King Louis then weighed in, offering Warwick lands in France if he overthrew Edward. In 1469 Warwick engineered

1461–1470 & 1471–1483

a series of uprisings beginning in the north of England and in July that year issued a proclamation demanding that Edward 'reform his ways' or be deposed. Edward found himself trapped at Nottingham by a rebel army. A relief force was sent that allowed him to escape but he realised a battle was out of the question and surrendered to Warwick. With the king imprisoned, Warwick sought to govern in his name but found little support in parliament or in the population at large. While Elizabeth Woodville was largely disliked, Edward was a highly popular monarch and Warwick could not risk raising the anger of the citizens of England and Edward was released.

Warwick now threw his support by the Lancastrians and led another rebellion in the autumn of 1470. Caught unawares and outnumbered, Edward fled to Flanders, and Henry VI was freed from the Tower and restored – briefly – to the throne. Edward's brother-in-law, Charles, Duke of Burgundy now felt compelled to provide Edward with a fleet and an army, and on 11 March 1471, Edward returned to England and defeated (and killed) Warwick at the Battle of Barnet on Easter Sunday.

In triumph, Edward marched to London and was restored to the throne. To ensure that there were no further uprisings in favour of Henry VI, he ordered him to be murdered. In 1475, Edward sought to regain the former English lands in France, but this time though the promise of support from his brother-in-law the Duke of Burgundy was not made good, and Edward was forced negotiate peace with King Louis. Edward's brothers Richard (later Richard III) and George saw this as an ignominious defeat, and George (who still harboured ambitions to be king himself) began to plot against Edward. This time, Edward had his brother arrested and executed, drowned, according to Shakespeare, in a butt of malmsey wine in February 1478.

In the last years of his reign, now secure on the throne from domestic and foreign threats, Edward fell victim to his own vices of sex and food. He gorged until he became obese and his health began to fail: just before his 41st birthday, Edward succumbed to pneumonia – although it is possible he had contracted typhoid or was even poisoned – and died. Edward's heir was still a child so Richard, Duke of Gloucester was appointed Lord High Protector. Young Edward V was far from being in safe hands, and Gloucester's treachery would ensure that he would never be crowned.

Elizabeth Woodville bore Edward ten children. Her daughter Elizabeth married Henry VII and she lived long enough to see her grandson, the future Henry VIII.

EDWARD V 1483

Nicknames: None known
Dynasty: House of York
Born: Abbot's House, Westminster on
2 November 1470
Succeeded to Throne: 9 April 1483 (deposed 25 June 1483)
Crowned at: Uncrowned
Died: Tower of London in late August/early September 1483

Buried: At the Tower of London, re-interred in the 17th century in Westminster Abbey
Authority: King of England and Wales, ruling Calais and parts of Ireland
Parents: Edward IV and Elizabeth Woodville
Married: Unmarried
Children: None

Little is known about Prince Edward, the heir of Edward IV. Instead, many gallons of ink have been spilled speculating on his fate and that of his younger brother, Richard. Sadly, it is almost certain that like several other Plantagenet princes, their lives were cut short by the actions of overly ambitious relatives.

Born within the confines of Westminster Abbey in 1470, where his mother was sheltering from the Lancastrian forces, Edward V succeeded his father at the age of 12 but was never crowned. In his fathers' will, the boy's uncle Richard, Duke of Gloucester was named as Protector. On 4 May, the young king and his younger brother Richard arrived in London from their home at Ludlow Castle and arrangements were made for Edward's coronation for 22 June. Sometime around 10 June, Edward and Richard were declared illegitimate. The Bishop of Bath and Wells revealed to Gloucester that Edward IV had married the prince's mother Elizabeth Woodville when he was already betrothed (betrothal meant in legal terms Edward was already married) to Lady Eleanor Butler. When parliament met it agreed that the prince and heir were 'bastards' and agreed to the succession to the throne of Richard, Duke of Gloucester as Richard III.

The two boys, who were lodged in the Tower of London, were seen infrequently in the summer of 1483 and then they disappeared completely. Over the centuries it came to be believed that, in the Bloody Tower, the princes were murdered by their uncle before their bodies were buried in the White Tower. A more recent theory is that the 'Princes in the Tower' were murdered by Henry VII (who defeated Richard III in 1485 at Bosworth) and then embarked on a campaign to blacken his name. In 1674 two skeletons of what appeared to be young boys were discovered in the White Tower and while forensic scientists examined them in 1933, their true identity has never been established.

RICHARD III

1483–1485

Although king for barely two years, Richard III came to epitomise evil, largely thanks to the writings of historians, the propaganda spread by the first Tudor king Henry VII, and later playwrights – most notably William Shakespeare. Thanks to Shakespeare, in most people's minds, Richard was the hunchback usurper to the throne who murdered the 'Princes in the Tower'. In fact Richard was tall and lean with slender limbs – the 'crouchback' or 'hunchback' appears to have been invented by Shakespeare to stand as a visual metaphor for wickedness – and there is no real evidence to support the claim that he killed Edward V and his brother in the Tower (he was out of London at the time), even though he had proclaimed them to be illegitimate in order to seize the throne.

There were clearly two sides to Richard's character: he was ruthlessly ambitious and skilled in the arts of deception, but, he treated his subjects fairly and governed well. Under Edward IV, Richard had been endowed with extensive states in the north of England, and was appointed Governor of the North. When he seized the throne, he was an experienced and able administrator and became highly regarded as a monarch by both the English and other European rulers. He was also a pious man, a firm supporter of the church who railed against poor morals and manners, and furthermore, was loyal to his wife, Anne Neville whom he had known since childhood, even though he had fathered several illegitimate children before their marriage in 1472.

Once secure on the throne Richard had to deal with the remaining Lancastrian opposition: the main threat came from his once loyal friend, Henry Stafford, Duke of Buckingham, who had allied himself with the Woodvilles (Edward IV's 'in-laws') and Henry Tudor, who through his mother Margaret Beaufort, was yet another descendent of Edward III and the last Lancastrian claimant to the English throne. In 1483 Buckingham launched a revolt but it was poorly organised and apparently halted in its tracks by a heavy hailstorm. Stafford was captured without a battle and executed at Salisbury. Meanwhile, Henry Tudor was safely in Brittany, waiting his opportunity.

Mid-way through his reign, in 1484 personal tragedies struck Richard: in April his son Edward, always a sickly child, died aged eight. Anne, who had consumption (TB), was too weak to bear other children

RICHARD III   1483-1485

Nicknames: *Richard Crookback, 'Old Dick'*

Dynasty: *House of York*

Born: *Fortheringhay Castle,
Northants on 2 October 1452*

Succeeded to Throne: *26 June 1483*

Crowned at: *Westminster Abbey on 6 July
1483*

Died: *Bosworth Field, Leicestershire
on 22 August 1485*

Buried: *Abbey of the Grey Friars, Leicester*

Authority: *King of England and Wales, ruling
Calais and parts of Ireland*

Parents: *Richard, 3rd Duke of York and Lady
Cecily Neville, their fourth surviving
son.*

Married: *Anne Neville (1456-85) daughter of
Warwick the Kingmaker on 12 July
1472 at Westminster Abbey.*

Children: *Edward, Prince of Wales (1473–84)*

After the Battle of Bosworth Field in August 1485, Richard's crown was discovered under a bush and presented to Henry Tudor.

and she died in March 1485. Another rumour spread was that Richard had her poisoned so he could marry his niece Elizabeth of York. This never happened: Richard may indeed have planned such a union after Anne's death to gain an heir, or perhaps to thwart Henry Tudor (who married Elizabeth in 1487).

Henry Tudor finally made his move in August 1485 and his army met Richard's at Market Bosworth, west of Leicester. Had Richard won this battle and lived, his authority to rule would have been unchallenged. Intent on killing Henry Tudor himself, Richard was himself slain – the last English king to die in battle – and his naked body carried on a packhorse to Leicester for burial. According to legend, Richard's crown was found on the battlefield under a hawthorn bush.

Richard III and his queen, Anne Neville, probably in their coronation robes. Richard was crowned on 6 July 1483.

HOUSE OF TUDOR 1485–1603

In an ironic twist of fate, the successor to the English throne after Richard III's death at Bosworth, was of Welsh descent. Henry Tudor – or Tudur to give in its Welsh spelling – was the grandson of Owain Tudur, a squire who claimed descent from the ancient independent princes of Wales. The advent of the Tudor dynasty marked a the end of the Middle Ages in England. With the Tudors came increasing peace, for the nobility had become so weakened during the Wars of the Roses that the Tudors were able to assert much more power than their Plantagenet forebears.

THE AGE OF DISCOVERY

Even though the five Tudor monarchs were not always popular (and in some instances were quite detested) they did a great deal to restore national pride to the nation. Trade and prosperity enabled social mobility, so the country was governed for the first time by the bright sons of butchers and farmers. The English wool trade continued to prosper and challenged Flanders' long domination of the cloth trade. Tudor expansionist plans were no longer the ancestral lands of Normandy: their eyes were set on more distant horizons, for this was the age of the great voyages of discovery of Columbus and Cabot, Magellan and Pizarro. The great mapmaker Mercator would complete the first map of the world and the English 'sea dogs' Drake and Raleigh would compete with their Spanish rivals for supremacy of the high seas. In this era Portugal established a trading link with India, while in England, Elizabeth I granted the first charter to the East India Company. English expansion overseas would not only bring new lands and colonies, but new species of plants – potatoes, tobacco, cocoa, strawberries and tomatoes amongst many others – would alter the diets and habits of Englishmen in centuries to come.

THE AGE OF DISSENT

The Tudor era was not without turmoil: religious upheaval and intolerance marked 16th century Europe. Catholicism was pitted against the new Protestantism, out of which would grow the Church of England following Henry VIII's break with Rome. Under Henry 3,000 monasteries- which not only housed monks, but were the sites of many artistic workshops (painting, illuminated manuscripts, stained glass and textiles), of medical and herbal knowledge, and also of often quite large scale industries (particularly brewing). But Martin Luther, who had ushered in the Reformation when he nailed his theses to the church door at Wittenberg in 1517, would be condemned as a heretic and William Tyndale, who produced a translation of the New Testament in English in 1543, along with some 300 Protestant martyrs, was burnt at the stake on the orders of the Catholic queen 'Bloody Mary'.

1485–1603

THE BOOK OF COMMON PRAYER

When Elizabeth came to the throne she had to deal with a country divided by religious hatred. She did not want revenge against Catholics, but nor did she want the iconoclastic zeal of Edward VI. Instead, she sought a balance in order to accommodate both creeds, so while Protestantism became the 'national religion' she did not think it wrong if Catholics wished to take the Roman mass in private. Elizabeth re-introduced the Book of Common Prayer (first published in 1552) for use by the Church of England and although there were 'Popish plots' against her (including Mary, Queen of Scots arrival in England in 1568), the earlier persecution of Protestants by her sister Mary Tudor were a propaganda gift to the anti-Catholics, and were made all the more potent by images of burnings at the stake that were reproduced in books such as Foxe's *Book of Martyrs* (published in 1563). Such images helped to fix a lasting fear of Roman Catholicism in many English minds.

THE NINE-DAYS QUEEN

In the struggle to continue the Protestant faith in England, the 16-year-old Lady Jane Grey was a victim of the scheming of her ambitious father-in-law, John Dudley, Duke of Northumberland. Jane was the granddaughter of Mary, Henry VIII's sister, and under his will, Mary's descendents had the right to the crown only after the death of his children and their heirs. Shortly before his death, Edward VI was persuaded by Northumberland to sign an amendment to his father's will that passed over six legitimate claimants to the throne in favour of Jane. Once Edward was dead, Northumberland then tried to kidnap the heir with the strongest claim – the Catholic Lady Mary, who was the eldest child of Henry VIII. Jane was secretly proclaimed queen on 10 July 1553, insisting that her husband Lord Guilford Dudley, was not jointly named king, and was lodged in the royal quarters in the Tower of London. Although a Protestant succession was ensured through Jane, Northumberland had underestimated the support for Mary from the English and the nobles. Jane was 'queen' for just nine days, and never formally crowned. Northumberland's army was defeated and he was captured and executed. Jane and Guilford were arrested and imprisoned in the Tower. Seeing that Jane's position had not been of her own making, Mary was prepared to spare her (and Guilford), but Jane's death warrant was sealed when her father, the Duke of Suffolk became involved in Sir Thomas Wyatt's plot to overthrow Mary. Jane refused to recant her Protestantism and on 12 February 1554 she was executed.

Sir Francis Drake, Elizabethan adventurer.

Lady Jane Grey, briefly queen of England.

Martin Luther, German religious reformer.

HENRY VII   1485–1509

Nicknames: None known

Dynasty: House of Tudor

Born: Pembroke Castle, Wales on 28 January 1457

Succeeded to Throne: 22 August 1485

Crowned at: Westminster Abbey on 30 October 1485

Died: Richmond Palace, Surrey on 21 April 1509

Buried: Henry VII's Chapel, Westminster Abbey

Authority: King of England and Wales, ruling Calais and parts of Ireland

Parents: Edmund Tudor, 1st Earl of Richmond and Margaret Beaufort (great-grand-daughter of Edward III, their only child.

Married: Elizabeth of York (1466-1503), eldest daughter of Edward IV, at Westminster Abbey on 18 January 1486

Children: Four surviving: Arthur (1486-1502), Henry VIII, Margaret (1489-1541) and Mary (1496-1533)

1485–1509

The first monarch of the Tudor dynasty, Henry VII was the son of the Lancastrian Earl of Richmond, Edmund Tudor (whose parents were the Welshman Owain Tudor and Catherine, widow of Henry V) and the Plantagenet Margaret Beaufort, through whom he claimed the throne and which was won at the Battle of Bosworth when Richard III was defeated. By marrying Edward IV's daughter, Elizabeth of York, Henry consolidated his position as king and united the Houses of York and Lancaster. Yet Henry would always remain a nervous and superstitious king, living by his wits and trusting no-one: he had Edward, Earl of Warwick (Richard III's nephew) executed in 1499 and similarly dispatched two further claimants, Lambert Simnel and Perkin Warbeck (who 'claimed' to be the youngest of the 'Princes in the Tower').

Henry was also determined to break the power of the barons who had been the source and the cause of so much conflict in the recent past. In 1487 Henry established the Star Chamber, named after the ceiling decorations of the room in the Place of Westminster where it met. This was a civil and criminal court of 20–30 judges that tried the barons if they broke the law and also banned them from raising private armies. With peace and order restored to England, Henry began to use the system of taxation, rents and feudal dues to rebuild the Crown's treasury.

In addition to treaties signed with the Netherlands, Spain and Portugal that were commercially advantageous to England, Henry was keen to make strong political alliances and in 1499, his son Arthur was married to Catherine, the daughter of Ferdinand and Isabella, the rulers of Aragon who had sponsored Columbus's discovery of the New World. Henry's own interests in trade and exploration (and no doubt seeing the competition from his European counterparts) led him to sponsor the Genoese sailor Giovanni Caboto (John Cabot) who set sail from Bristol in 1497 and 'discovered' Newfoundland – some 500 years after the Vikings.

1485–1509

Fearful of expensive wars, Henry sought an alliance with England's old foe the French, key to which was an alliance with Scotland. Negotiations began in 1487 but the Scottish king James III's friendly stance angered many north of the border and led to his murder in 1488. It was not until 1502 that a peace treaty between England and Scotland was finally signed, and was reinforced the following year when Henry's daughter Margaret married the Scottish king James IV. Furthermore, as Henry's reign progressed, many members of the Welsh nobility were granted senior posts and lands in Wales so that English domination lessened. For the first time in generations there was peace between England, Scotland and Wales.

Henry's final years were marked by personal sadness: his eldest son Arthur died in 1502 (aged only 15) and Henry's wife Elizabeth died in childbirth in 1503. Henry retreated into private life: he ordered the rebuilding of Sheen Palace (badly damaged by fire in 1497): it emerged from the ashes as the fabulous Richmond Palace, to where he retired as his health began to fail.

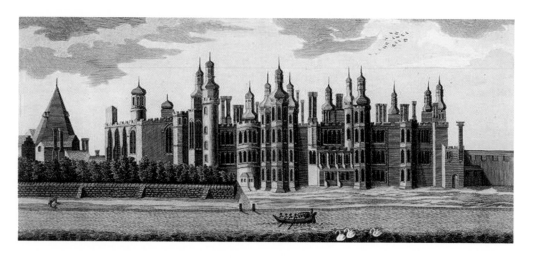

A view of Richmond Palace published in 1765.

Elizabeth of York, Henry VII's queen.

HENRY VIII 1509–1547

Nicknames: *Bluff King Hal (posthumous); the 'Father of the English Navy'*

Dynasty: *House of Tudor*

Born: *Greenwich Palace, Kent, on 28 June 1491*

Succeeded to Throne: *22 April 1509*

Crowned at: *Westminster Abbey on 24 June 1509*

Died: *St. James's Palace, London on 28 January 1547*

Buried: *St. George's Chapel, Windsor Castle, Berkshire*

Authority: *King of England and Ireland (from 1542), Calais and Boulogne (from 1544), Tournai (1513–19)*

Parents: *Henry VII and Elizabeth of York, their second son.*

Children: *Mary I (by Catherine of Aragon), Elizabeth (by Anne Boleyn), Edward VI (by Jane Seymour), and a natural son, Henry Fitzroy (with mistress, Elizabeth Blount) died 1536, aged about 20.*

1509-1547

WIVES OF HENRY VIII

(1) Catherine of Aragon (1485-1536) daughter of King Ferdinand II of Spain on 11 June 1509 at the Chapel of the Observant Friars. Divorced May 1533.
(2) Anne Boleyn (1507-36) daughter of Sir Thomas Boleyn, on 25 January 1533, secretly at Whitehall Place. Beheaded for infidelity on 19 May 1536.
(3) Jane Seymour (1508–37), daughter of Sir John Seymour, on 30 May 1536 at Queen's Closet, Whitehall Palace. Died 24 October 1537

(4) Anne of Cleves (1515–57), second daughter of John, Duke of Cleves, on 6 January 1540 at Greenwich Palace. Divorced July 1540.
(5) Catherine Howard (c.1520–42), daughter of Lord Edmund Howard, on 28 July 1540 at Oatlands manor house in Surrey. Beheaded for adultery on 13 February 1542.
(6) Catherine Parr (c.1512–48), daughter of Sir Thomas Parr, on 12 July 1543 at Hampton Court Palace.

On the death of his older brother Arthur in 1502, Henry, Duke of York, became the heir to the throne and succeeded as king in 1509. The young Henry is best described as a 'Renaissance Man': sportsman (a keen 'real' tennis player with courts installed at Hampton Court Palace), dancer, musician (the song Greensleeves has long been attributed to him) a master of French and Latin and fluent in Italian and Spanish, Henry was also particularly interested in theology. While many argue that Henry was England's most important king because of the wealth and status he brought to the kingdom as well as the establishment of the Church of England, for most he remains most famous for his six wives.

Henry's first wife was his brother Arthur's widow, Catherine of Aragon, a union to which Henry agreed in order to maintain the alliance with Spain. Henry and Catherine were married on 11 June 1509 and two weeks later were crowned at Westminster Abbey.

Henry's interest in foreign affairs led him to appoint trusted ministers to deal with the day-to-day affairs of government: chief among his ministers were William Warham, Archbishop of Canterbury; Thomas Howard, the Lord Treasurer; Bishop Richard Foxe and later, in 1514, Thomas Wolsey. He rid the court of Edmund Dudley and Sir Richard Empson who, under Henry VII, had introduced stringent and deeply unpopular taxes. They were executed for 'constructive treason' in 1510. He began to develop the navy, building some of the finest ships of the age including the Mary Rose. In June 1513 Henry led an invasion force to Calais knowing that James IV of Scotland would take the opportunity of his absence to invade England. Henry sent Thomas Howard to counter the Scots and at the Battle of Flodden on 9 September 1513, James and the 'flower of Scottish nobility' were killed.

1509–1547

Meanwhile, Henry was equally victorious in France at Therouanne and Tournai and famously at the Battle of the Spurs on 16 August 1513 – the name of the battle signifying the speed of retreat of the French troops. Wolsey negotiated the peace and one of the conditions was the marriage of Henry's sister Mary to Louis XII of France in August 1514: a short-lived union as Louis died two months later, Mary then angered her brother by secretly marrying his close friend Charles Brandon, Duke of Suffolk. They were eventually pardoned and subsequently were the grandparents of the unfortunate Lady Jane Grey. Henry was determined to be centre stage in Europe and when the Holy Roman Emperor Maximilian I died in 1519, Henry tried to succeed him. But his European ambitions were to be thwarted: the electors selected another Hapsburg, Charles V, to succeed Maximilian and his attempts to have Wolsey made Pope came to nought. The most significant event in Europe that was to affect England was the action of the reformer Martin Luther who began an attack on the Papacy and the Catholic Church in 1517. Henry went to the defence of the pope, countering Luther's tract *On the Babylonish Captivity of the Church* (1520) with his own *Defence of the Seven Sacraments* (co-written with Thomas More and John Fisher) that became a best-seller throughout Europe. In recognition of this support, in 1521 Pope Leo X named Henry *Fidei Defensor* ('Defender of the Faith'), a title used by all subsequent English monarchs, although that would soon seem inappropriate for Henry himself.

Henry needed a son and heir, and while Catherine had borne him six children, only one daughter, Mary, survived infancy. In 1526, Catherine was about 40 years old and it was clear that a son would never be born. Extremely concerned about the inheritance and what became known as 'the king's great matter', Henry used the excuse that he had sinned against the church by marrying his dead brother's widow – even though the union had a papal blessing. Furthermore, in 1519 Henry's mistress Elizabeth Blount had given birth to a boy, Henry Fitzroy, and although illegitimate, Henry began to think of the boy as a possible heir. In 1527 Henry became infatuated with Anne Boleyn (whose sister Mary was also one of the king's mistresses). Anne shrewdly held out against the King's amorous advances and Wolsey began the lengthy negotiations with Pope Clement VII to have Henry's marriage annulled.

Clement procrastinated for six years and during this time many countries began to break with Rome and introduce Lutherism. Wolsey, unable to make headway fell from power and was arrested in 1530. Henry's new adviser Thomas Cromwell advised a split with Rome and in 1534 the Act of Supremacy, acknowledged Henry as head of the separate Church of England with the power to appoint his own archbishops and bishops. Thomas Cranmer, the new Archbishop of Canterbury pronounced Henry's marriage to Catherine void in May 1533, but Henry had secretly married Anne in January when she was already one month pregnant. The Pope threatened – but never carried out – excommunication.

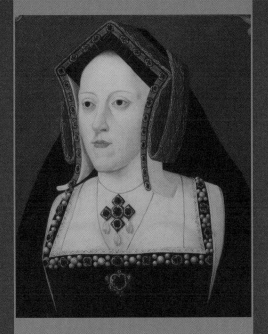

Catherine of Aragon, Henry VIII's first wife and the mother of Mary Tudor.

Cardinal Thomas Wolsey enriched himself during his political career, and built Hampton Court Palace.

Anne Boleyn, mother of Queen Elizabeth I.

Anne of Cleves, Henry's fourth wife.

The court of Henry VIII.

Catherine Parr, who survived Henry.

1509-1547

Henry's relationship with Anne was suffering: she bore him a daughter (the future Elizabeth I) but no sons as each subsequent pregnancy ended in stillbirths. Once again Henry went a-courting, and to dispense with Anne, trumped up charges of incest (with her brother) adultery with four lovers, attempted murder and hinted at witchcraft. She was beheaded in 1536. His illegitimate son Henry Fitzroy also died in 1536. Henry's third wife, married just one month later, was Jane Seymour. When Jane died just a year later in 1537 having borne him a longed-for son, Henry was grief stricken but he had to deal with an uprising in the north, the Pilgrimage of Grace, in which thousands of Catholics demanded a 'return to the church of Rome'. Henry had more than 200 rebels executed. Although Henry was now head of his own church in his dominions, he nevertheless attempted to reassure his Catholic subjects by publishing the Act of the Six Articles (1539) that reaffirmed doctrines inherited from Rome. Any dissenters who would not support Henry in this role, such as Thomas More and Bishop John Fisher, were executed. Henry's next move was on the monasteries, which had become wealthy, powerful and resistant to change, and in 1539 Henry dissolved them and confiscated their lands and properties.

In 1540 at Cromwell's urging, Henry married for a fourth time to a Protestant princess, Anne of Cleves. The portrait of her by Hans Holbein that had been sent to Henry was apparently 'over-flattening': it is said that upon meeting her in the flesh, Henry asked Anne's retinue why they had sent him a 'Flemish Mare' and not a princess. Although they married at Greenwich in January 1540, the marriage was never consummated, both parties agreed to a divorce (in July 1540) and Anne and Henry remained good friends. Henry, now aged 48 and overweight was now smitten with the 19 year old Catherine Howard and they were married in July 1540, three weeks after his divorce from Anne of Cleves. While Henry delighted in his beautiful teenage bride, Catherine soon tired of the king: she was accused of adultery, betrayed by her friends, charged with treason and executed in February 1542.

Henry's last marriage was to an older woman, the twice-widowed Catherine Parr. In her, Henry found a companion, an intellectual equal and a loving stepmother to his three surviving children, Mary, Elizabeth and Edward. The following year, Henry decided that if his son Edward (who was a sickly boy) left no children, he would be succeeded by Mary, and then if necessary, by Elizabeth. By this stage, Henry's health was deteriorating rapidly: grossly overweight and in agonies from ulcers on his legs, he had to be pushed around in a specially constructed handcart. Henry VIII, the creator of the modern English state and the first king to be called 'Your Majesty', died in 1547 aged 55. He was buried at Windsor next to Jane Seymour, the wife who had borne him a much-longed for son and heir.

EDWARD VI

1547–1553

Born on the eve of the Feast of St Edward the Confessor (hence his name), Edward VI was a weak, sick and short-sighted child who, in order to protect him, was lodged at Hampton Court Palace where his food was routinely checked for poison and (remarkably for the 16th century) strict hygiene controls were required by his attendants. Educated as a Protestant, Edward was only nine years old when he succeeded to the throne. Too young to rule, a council of regency was called and appointed Edward's uncle, Edward Seymour, Earl of Hertford and Duke of Somerset, as Protector of the Realm.

Seymour was leader of the Reform faction in the regency council and was supported by Archbishop Cranmer and John Dudley, Earl of Warwick. Seymour and Cranmer altered the Coronation Oath to commit the king firmly to the Reformation and as their rule continued, the council ordered church services to be held in English and not Latin, and the removal of all 'popish' images. This resulted in much of the finest medieval art in England being destroyed: stained glass windows and sculptures were smashed, tapestries ripped and murals painted over; mystery plays and maypoles were banned; Catholic altars were replaced by communion tables and the clergy allowed (even encouraged) to marry.

In domestic politics, the council increased the pace of land enclosure that ended the medieval farming practices that allowed common land to be used for grazing. Enclosures dispossessed many peasant farmers and led to serious rebellions, notably Kett's Rebellion in 1549. Seymour was overthrown and was arrested by the regency council.

Warwick was now in charge and governed the country effectively, winning Edward's trust and earning himself the title Duke of Northumberland. In 1552 the young king caught measles and smallpox and by the spring of the following year it was clear that he was dying. He quickly drafted a plan for the succession that passed over his two half-sisters – he especially didn't want the Catholic Mary on the throne – and at Northumberland's urging, named the unfortunate Lady Jane Grey who could be trusted to carry on with the plans for Reformation, as his successor. Edward died, evidently praying that England should not revert to Catholicism, but his death was kept secret while Northumberland moved to install Jane as queen.

EDWARD VI 1547–1553

Nicknames: *None known*
Dynasty: *House of Tudor*
Born: *Hampton Court Palace, Surrey,*
on 12 October 1537
Succeeded to Throne: *28 January 1547*
Crowned at: *Westminster Abbey*
on 19 February 1547
Died: *Greenwich Palace, Kent on 6 July 1553*

Buried: *Henry VII's Chapel, Westminster Abbey*
Authority: *King of England and Ireland,*
Calais and Boulogne (until 1551)
Parents: *Henry VIII and Jane Seymour,*
their only child.
Married: *Unmarried*
Children: *None*

MARY I 1533-1558

Nicknames: Bloody Mary
Dynasty: House of Tudor
Born: Greenwich Palace, Kent
on 8 February 1516
Proclaimed Queen: 19 July 1553
Crowned at: Westminster Abbey
on 1 October 1553
Died: St. James's Palace, London
on 17 November 1558
Buried: Henry VII's Chapel, Westminster Abbey

Authority: Queen of England, Ireland
and Calais
Parents: Henry VIII and Catherine of Aragon,
their only surviving child.
Married: Prince Philip II of Spain (1527–98),
son of Emperor Charles V, on 25 July
1554 at Winchester Cathedral.
(Philip was given the courtesy title
King of England)
Children: None

1533–1558

Edward VI's half-sister, the staunchly Catholic Mary was the eldest child of Henry VIII and the product of his marriage to Catherine of Aragon. She was in Norfolk when Northumberland was manoeuvring Lady Jane Grey onto the throne. Gathering an army, Mary marched on London and was greeted by popular support as the rightful heir to the throne. Mary was the first formally anointed Queen of England (neither Matilda, the daughter of Henry I who succeed in 1135, nor Jane Grey were ever crowned). Her inevitable restoration of the Catholic faith in England met with little opposition – although some 800 Protestants did flee abroad – as did her act to invalidate her father's divorce from her mother that restored her own legitimacy and made her half-sister Elizabeth a bastard.

But Mary's plan to overturn the Act of Supremacy that would have returned England to obedience to the pope was fiercely resisted. So too was her plan to marry Philip of Spain, son and heir to the powerful and Catholic Holy Roman Emperor Charles V. This affront to English 'nationalism' and independence provoked an armed uprising in Kent in 1554 led by Sir Thomas Wyatt, which was defeated and saw Wyatt sent to the executioner's block. Philip of Spain arrived in England in 1554, he and Mary were married in Winchester Cathedral. Mary was by now 38 and appropriately for a queen, still a virgin; Philip was 27, highly sexed and very experienced, but preferred the ladies of the court to his wife. In November 1555 Cardinal Pole, the papal legate formally announced that England was restored to Rome and the Holy See, but with this came the papal demand that all heretics must be burned at the stake.

So began the moment of Mary's 'bloody' reign of terror. Over the next three years, more than 300 Protestants were sent to their deaths. Among them were Thomas Cranmer, Archbishop of Canterbury (who was replaced by Cardinal Pole); Hugh Latimer, Bishop of Winchester, and Nicholas Ridley, Bishop of London. Naturally enough there were now plots to overthrow Mary: in December 1555, the 'Dudley Conspiracy' (named after its chief plotter Sir Henry Dudley) planned to rob the Exchequer, overthrow Mary and place her half-sister Elizabeth on the throne. News of the plot leaked and most of the conspirators were caught or fled to France.

In 1555 Philip left England for Spain, where, in 1556 he became king (and Mary, queen). He returned only once for a few weeks in 1557, enough time for Mary to convince herself that she was pregnant but it turned out to be a 'false pregnancy'. Mary remained unpopular, partly because of the ill-advised war against France in 1558. Mary was urged by Philip to back Spain in this campaign, the result of which was the loss of Calais, England's last and only French territory. The loss was a huge blow to English pride. 'When I am dead you will find Calais engraved on my heart', said Mary.

Heartbroken by both the loss of Calais and the prolonged absence of Philip, who Mary clearly loved, and her health weakened by influenza, Mary once again convinced herself that she was pregnant. Indeed her belly was swollen, but she in fact was suffering from cancer of the stomach and was dying. Shortly before her death she reluctantly accepted that her 'bastard' half-sister Elizabeth should succeed her.

ELIZABETH I

1558–1603

The only surviving child of Henry VIII and Anne Boleyn, Elizabeth was less than three years old when her mother was executed and she was sent to live at Hatfield Palace in Hertfordshire. She was declared illegitimate and her position fluctuated several times during the turbulent years of her youth. She was a potential focus for plotters during her siblings' reigns and it is down to luck and shrewdness on her part that she escaped with her life.

Like her father, Elizabeth was extremely well educated: she could read and write in English, Latin and several other languages. She was raised a Protestant, which aroused the immediate distrust of her sister Mary, who believed that Elizabeth was plotting against her. Imprisoned in the Tower of London and later at Woodstock, near Oxford, Elizabeth returned to Hatfield after being reconciled with her sister in 1555, but Mary's death must have come as a great relief.

Elizabeth's first act as queen was to appoint her trusted friend and adviser William Cecil, later Lord Burghley as her secretary, and he would remain her chief minister for the next 40 years. The persecution of Protestants stopped immediately and careful not to create a backlash against Catholics (although most were purged from the royal council) she tried to strike a balance, allowing Catholics to take mass in private. Famously, she 'had no desire to make windows into men's souls'.

There would nevertheless continue to be Catholic plots against her, particularly after 1570 when the pope issued a bull deposing her. Elizabeth responded exactly as her father had done and ignored the pope. Much against her wishes, though, persecution of Catholics resumed which in turn led to tensions with Scotland. Elizabeth's treatment of her cousin and claimant on the English throne, Mary, Queen of Scots cast a dark shadow over her reign. Imprisoned for 20 years in England, Mary was the focus for Catholic plots and Elizabeth hesitated over her fate. Eventually – and reluctantly – she signed her death warrant in 1587.

Marriage was an overriding concern for much of her reign. Elizabeth's ministers pleaded with her to marry and provide an heir, and while she entertained several suitors, her position as 'Virgin Queen' and the most powerful woman in Europe was not one she was prepared to relinquish. Besides, England was prosperous, relatively peaceful and Elizabeth was hugely popular with her subjects. Cleverly, Elizabeth used the many proposals from continental suitors – Phillip II of Spain, Erik XIV of Sweden, a pair of Hapsburg dukes and Francois, Duke of Alencon and son of Henry II of France – to keep the Catholic rulers in Europe guessing about her intentions and stop them interfering with affairs in England. She was also close to Robert Dudley Earl of Leicester, but

ELIZABETH I   1558–1603

Nicknames: *The Virgin Queen,*
Good Queen Bess, Gloriana
Dynasty: *House of Tudor*
Born: *Greenwich Palace, Kent*
on 7 September 1533
Succeeded to Throne: *17 November*
1558
Crowned at: *Westminster Abbey*
on 15 January 1559

Died: *Richmond Palace, Surrey*
on 24 March 1603
Buried: *Henry VII's Chapel, Westminster Abbey*
Authority: *Queen of England, Ireland,*
and Virginia (1587–91)
Parents: *Henry VIII and Anne Boleyn,*
their only child.
Married: *Unmarried*
Children: *None*

The Spanish Armada was destroyed in storms off the English coast.

Mary, Queen of Scots fled to England in 1568 after her abdication. She remained Elizabeth's prisoner for 19 years, until her involvement in the Babington Plot led to her execution for treason.

Robert Dudley, Earl of Leicester was widely believed to be Elizabeth's lover.

marriage to him was politically impossible. Making the most of England's adoration of her, Elizabeth made her accession day (17 November) a national holiday and she toured the country on 'progresses' so the people could see her. Her majestic appearance and fashionable clothes no doubt made her a fantastic sight to behold, and even after she contracted smallpox in 1562 that left her scarred and bald, she maintained her appearance with wigs and cosmetics at her courts at Whitehall, Greenwich, Richmond, Hampton Court and Windsor.

In the 1580s England was drawn inextricably into war with Spain, in part caused by rebellion in the Netherlands, which was vital to English trade, and partly by the execution of Mary, Queen of Scots in 1587. Philip II of Spain felt compelled to return England to the 'true Church', especially as Francis Drake and other English 'pirates' were preying on Spanish ships. In 1587, Drake 'singed the King of Spain's beard' with an attack on Cadiz and the following year, he took a leading role in the defeat of the Spanish Armada, the fleet of 130 vessels sent to invade England. Elizabeth's troops mustered at Tilbury to defend London, where she made her famous speech declaring that 'I know I have the body of a week and feeble woman, but I have the heart and stomach of a king, and a king of England too.' The subsequent Spanish defeat was hailed as 'divine deliverance', even though it was the English weather that halted the Spanish invasion: a fierce westerly gale forced many of the Spanish ships north to Scotland and Ireland where many were wrecked.

In her fifties, Elizabeth developed an affection for the young and charming Robert Devereux, Earl of Essex who was given a series of military commands. Sent to Ireland to put down a rebellion, Essex made a truce with the earl of Tyrone (who was planning to install Philip II of Spain as King of Ireland) instead of defeating him. Elizabeth was furious and Essex was arrested. He attempted a coup in 1601 and eventually, paid with his head. In 1598, Elizabeth was 65 years old, she had lost beauty, her teeth and her hair, and she had outlived many of her trusted friends and advisors. Inflation gripped the economy after a succession of failed harvests, and high taxes needed to prosecute the war with Spain caused resentment. Nevertheless, in a speech to Parliament in 1601 that moved many members to tears, she demonstrated that she was still worthy of the her moniker of 'Good Queen Bess'. "And though you have had, and may have, many mightier and wiser princes sitting in this seat, yet you never had, nor shall have, any that will love you better."

When Elizabeth succeeded Mary in 1558 she began a 44-year reign that was without question, the most glorious England had ever seen. Pride in England – which she fostered and turned to her advantage – inspired some of the finest music, painting, and literature .Shakespeare played his part in the 'propaganda' by glorifying the Tudor dynasty in his plays, while in Edmund Spenser's *The Faerie Queen*, Elizabeth appeared as the beautiful and chaste Belphoebe, and as Gloriana, the majestic queen.

THE STUARTS
1603–1714

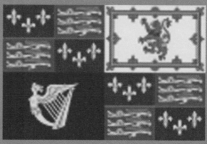

1603–49

1704-1714

The Stuart dynasty was the ruling house for most of the 17th century. When Elizabeth I died without an heir, the crown went to James VI of Scotland, a descendant of Henry VIII's sister Margaret. James, who had for reigned for 35 years in Scotland since the abdication of his mother Mary, Queen of Scots, was crowned James I of England in 1603. His accession united the two kingdoms that had for many centuries been sworn enemies. A Protestant, James was nonetheless tolerant of Catholics, and was even prepared to allow his son and heir Charles to be engaged to a Catholic princess.

KING JAMES BIBLE

James was fat, 'weak-kneed' and misshapen, and while well educated, he was stuttering and stumbling in speech – evidently his tongue too big for his mouth-and few could understand his Scottish accent. Nevertheless, it was during his reign that the Authorised Version of the Bible, commonly known as the 'King James Bible', was created. The Hampton Court Conference of 1605, a gathering of Anglicans and Puritans and chaired by the king, declared that there were far too many versions of the scriptures: there was the 1539 Great Bible by William Tyndale and Miles Coverdale, the 1560 Geneva Bible by English refugee Protestants in Switzerland (this was called the 'Breeches Bible' because it had Adam and Eve fashioning themselves breeches or trousers out of fig leaves) and the rival Bishop's Bible of 1572. James ordered these to be replaced with a single bible, translated by over 50 scholars working in six teams, reviewed by the bishops and ratified by the crown. The bible was published in 1611 – with a dedication to King James – and for centuries it remained the best-known translation in English-speaking countries.

THE GUNPOWDER PLOT

King James's reign had a difficult start: he did not have the charm of Elizabeth and was both suspicious and conceited. In Scotland he had ruled by the Divine Right of Kings and was not answerable to men: he had in 1599 even published his book, *Basilikon Doron* upholding his divine rights. But in England he found a parliament with power and authority that worked effectively as the government. This style of rule James found unacceptable and several time he dismissed parliament and ruled for long periods acting only on the advice of his friends. In his first years of rule he faced a number of conspiracies, with two plots to depose him in 1603. But the Gunpowder Plot was the most serious. James had been under pressure to grant Catholics greater toleration, something the king felt unable to do.

THE STUARTS

1603–1714

In May 1604, a group of conspirators led by Sir Robert Catesby, that included Guy Fawkes, had rented a house next door to parliament and had dug a tunnel through to the cellar underneath the House of Lords. They then rented a room above the cellar and filled it with barrels of gunpowder: the plot was to blow up the king at the state opening of parliament in November 1605. At this stage one of the conspirators became alarmed and warned his brother-in-law Lord Monteagle, a member of the House of Lords, to avoid the event. Monteagle alerted the Secretary of State who in turn, informed the king. A search of the House of Lords was ordered and at midnight Guy Fawkes was discovered in the cellar with the gunpowder. Soon the others were rounded up and all were sent to the Tower of London. James himself wrote the warrant allowing Fawkes to be tortured – gently at first and then *et sic per gradus ad ima tenditur*, 'and so on step by step to the limit' – before he was finally hanged, then drawn and quartered.

ROYAL PATRONAGE

Under the Stuarts the 17th century witnessed a flourishing of the arts and architecture. James commissioned numerous portraits from Flemish artists, as well as patronising the architect and stage designer Inigo Jones whose best known works include the Queens' House at Greenwich and the magnificent Banqueting House in Whitehall, which was built in 1619 to replace the recently burned down Whitehall Palace. Designed in a classical style, it was completed in 1622- although the magnificent interiors were not complete until 1635 under Charles I when the vast ceiling paintings by Peter Paul Rubens were installed. The Banqueting House would be the only building in the new palace to survive a second fire – the Great Fire of London in 1666. Charles I was, like his father, a great patron of the arts and was an admirer of the artist Anthony Van Dyke who was tempted to England by the offer of a knighthood and a pension. Charles II took a great interest in the architecture and science: he supported Christopher Wren's construction of St Paul's Cathedral and the naval hospital at Greenwich, and supported the foundation of the Royal Society in 1662 which would encourage the enquiries of Isaac Newton and Robert Boyle into chemistry and physics.

When William of Orange was 'invited' to Britain to replace James II, Dutch artists and designers were brought to Britain, while under Queen Anne, the last Stuart monarch, a distinctive taste emerged that was characterised by simple ornament and elegant lines, especially in furniture. John Vanburgh, the designer of Castle Howard in Yorkshire was also architect of Blenheim Palace, the house given to John Churchill, Duke of Marlborough by Queen Anne in gratitude for his victory over the French in 1704. Among the great craftsmen who worked with Vanburgh at Blenheim were the carver Grinling Gibbons and the architect Nicholas Hawksmoor.

Thomas Winter, executed in 1606 as one of the co-conspirators in the Gunpowder Plot.

The Banqueting Hall, Whitehall, was designed by Inigo Jones and its magnificent ceilings painted by Peter Paul Rubens.

133

The Civil War of the 17th century reduced the power of the monarchy, and set Britain on course for government by parliamentary democracy.

Oliver Cromwell, (1599–1658), nicknamed 'Old Ironside' by his troops, was an effective military leader, a Puritan and England's only republican head of state.

CIVIL WAR 1642–49

One of the greatest political upheavals in British history, the English Civil War broke out in the reign of Charles I. Its had its roots in the rivalry between parliament and the crown. Since the reign of Elizabeth I, parliament had grown in strength and evolved into an effective organ of government with the sole right to raise taxes. Charles I's autocratic rule – his absolute belief in his divine right to rule – put him at odds with parliament and reached a crisis in 1642 when the king attempted to have five members of parliament arrested. The men were forewarned and fled, but it was the opening shot in the Civil War.

Over the next seven years the country was split as Royalists and Parliamentarians clashed in sporadic battles. The first pitched battle at Edgehill in October 1642 was inconclusive, but with time, the forces of parliament became better organised. At the Battle of Naseby in 1645, a 15,000-strong New Model Army under Oliver Cromwell and Thomas Fairfax defeated a Royalist army half its size led by Charles I. Charles fled to Scotland but was handed over to Parliament in 1646: he escaped but was recaptured and imprisoned at Carisbroke Castle on the Isle of Wight where he negotiated for his freedom, at the same time arranging for a Scottish army to invade England. Cromwell again saw off the challenge at Preston in August 1648, leaving the king at the mercy of Parliament. In 1649 Parliament decided to try the king for waging war against his kingdom. The trial began on 20 January and lasted seven days, throughout which Charles refused to recognize the legality of the court. Found guilty Charles I was sentenced to death and was executed on the morning of 30 January on a specially erected scaffold in front of Banqueting House in Whitehall.

INTERREGNUM: THE COMMONWEALTH AND PROTECTORATE

The period between the execution of Charles I in 1649 and the restoration of his son Charles II to the throne in 1660 is generally divided into two parts: the Commonwealth (or Republic) which lasted from 1649–53 and the Protectorate, a monarchy in all but name under Oliver Cromwell and his son, Richard, from 1653–59. During the first period Cromwell instituted a system of republican government and ruled at first through the Rump Parliament comprised of the 53 Members of Parliament who had called for the trial of Charles I in 1649. When the Rump Parliament began to obstruct Cromwell's reforms, it was dissolved in 1653 and Cromwell became Lord Protector, ruling with a Council of 15 and a Parliament of 400 members.

During Cromwell's Protectorate English military skill was raised to new heights: Jamaica was taken from the Spanish and the Dutch were overwhelmed at sea, giving English ships the monopoly

1603–1714

over trade in and out of foreign ports, by the navy under the command of Robert Blake. In 1657 Cromwell refused an offer for him to be crowned king and after his death in 1659, his son Richard became Lord Protector but he resigned a year later. A new Parliament was called and in 1660 negotiated the restoration of the monarchy under Charles II who was in exile in Holland.

THE PLAGUE AND THE GREAT FIRE OF LONDON

On 7 June 1665, the great diarist of the age, Samuel Pepys noted in his diary that as he walked down Drury Lane he saw red crosses hastily painted on three front doors: these crossed marked the homes of those who had fallen ill with the deadly bubonic plague. By September more than 100,000 Londoners were dead. Unlike many of the wealthy, Charles II remained in London until August when he took up temporary residence in Salisbury. Six months after the king returned to London in the spring of 1666, disaster struck again: fire broke out in a bakery in Pudding Lane on 2 September and engulfed the building causing it to collapse and spread the flames along the whole street. The flames, fanned by easterly winds soon took hold of the largely timber-framed buildings stacked closely in the warren of street. For four days and three nights, London burned out of control until on 5 September, the wind dropped and the fire burned itself out.

In the meantime Charles and his brother James, Duke of York led gangs of men with picks and shovels to blow up or pull down buildings in the path of the flames to create firebreaks. When the Tower of London, the storehouse of the state's supply of gunpowder, was threatened, Charles ordered the demolition of houses between the western gates and City. Four-fifths of the City of London was destroyed: 13,000 houses and public buildings, among them the Royal Exchange, the Guildhall and the Customs House were beyond repair. The death toll has been put at about 12, but it is likely to have been higher, simply because many deaths of poor people were unrecorded. A column, known as The Monument, designed by Christopher Wren marks the fire's origins in Pudding Lane next to London Bridge.

Monument, an obelisk topped by a flaming gilded urn, marks the start of the fire.

The Great Fire of London lasted four days and consumed a large part of medieval London.

JAMES I   1603–1625
(JAMES VI OF SCOTLAND)

Nicknames: The 'wisest fool in Christendom';
the 'British Solomon'

Dynasty: House of Stuart

Born: Edinburgh Castle on 19 June 1566

Succeeded to Thrones:
24 July 1567 (Scotland)
and 24 March 1603 (England)

Crowned at:
Church of the Holy Rood, outside Stirling
Castle, Scotland on 29 July 1567, and
Westminster Abbey on 25 July 1603

Died: Theobalds Park, Hertfordshire
on 27 March 1625

Buried: St. George's Chapel,
Windsor Castle, Berkshire

Authority: King of Great Britain, Ireland, Virginia
(from 1607), New England (from
1620) and Bermuda (from 1609)

Parents: Mary, Queen of Scots (Mary Stuart)
and Henry Stuart, Lord Darnley,
their only child.

Married: Anne (1574–1619) daughter of
King Frederick II of Denmark on
20 August 1590 in Oslo, Norway.

Children: Seven, notably Henry, Prince of
Wales (1594–1612), Charles I, and
Elizabeth (1596–1622)

JAMES I (JAMES VI OF SCOTLAND)

1603–1625

James I of England was also James VI of Scotland and the first monarch to unite the crowns of England and Scotland. The son of Mary, Queen of Scots and Henry, Lord Darnley, James was descended from Henry VII and endured a miserable childhood which marked his character. With the murder of his father and the exile of his mother, he was effectively orphaned as a baby, and as the infant king of Scotland was the focus for plots and dissension. He was terrified of assassination and wore thickly padded clothes to protect his body and while his education left him with a lust for knowledge, it also gave him nightmares throughout the rest of his life.

Baptised a Catholic and raised a Protestant, when he ascended the throne in England, James worked for religious tolerance. He refrained from persecution of the Catholics, but was not as fervent a Protestant as either the members of the Scottish Kirk or the Calvinist English Puritans would have liked. Although James authorised a new version of the Bible, the Puritans were not satisfied and in 1620 the Pilgrim Fathers set sail for America on *The Mayflower*: the first English colony at Jamestown in Virginia had been established in 1607 by John Smith and by 1609, James's 'kingdom' in the New World extended to Bermuda. Meanwhile, Catholic dissenters to Protestant rule in England were planning to blow up Parliament – and the king – in the 1605 Gunpowder Plot.

Most problematic was James's attitude to parliament: James was convinced of his 'divine right to rule'- the doctrine under which kings were appointed by God and so not answerable to men. Disputes between the king and parliament led on several occasions to James dismissing parliament and ruling alone, relying on the advice of favourites. Chief among these were Robert Carr, a former page elevated to the earldom of Somerset in 1613, and later George Villiers, Duke of Buckingham from in 1616. Carr was a member of the Privy Council and entrusted with the King's most intimate affairs. It was he who urged the king to make the alliance with Spain and helped levy a number of dubious taxes.

In foreign affairs, James tried to establish strong Protestant alliances in Europe and to this end he married his daughter Elizabeth to Frederick, the Elector Palatine in 1613. However ,when Frederick became King of Bohemia in 1618, Europe was drawn into the Thirty Years War, and England was under pressure to support Bohemia against two of the greatest powers in Europe, the Hapsburg Austria and Spain.

Renowned for his intelligence and scholarship, James was the first king to travel under water: in 1620 Cornelius Drebbel, who as well as developing the thermometer and microscope, took James for a trip down the Thames in his 'submarine'. In the last 15 years of his reign, the king's health – both physical and mental – was beginning to fail, and this once knowledgeable monarch came increasingly under the domination of George Villiers. It was rumoured that the pair had a homosexual relationship. Nevertheless, when James died of kidney failure in 1625, he had reigned in Scotland and England for over 50 years.

CHARLES I

1625–49

Charles did not expect to become king – he only became heir to the throne on the death of his older brother Henry in 1612 – but like his father, he believed firmly in the Divine Right of Kings and was acutely aware of his dignity as monarch, insisting on great formality in his court. No one was allowed to sit in his presence and formal dining often occurred under the gaze of the public. His firm beliefs in his right to rule made him stubborn in his dealings with parliament, with whom he quarrelled constantly – and for 11 years he ruled without one – and it would eventually bring about his own death. Like his father too, Charles fell under the spell of George Villiers, Duke of Buckingham. When parliament sought to impeach Villiers in 1626, Charles dissolved parliament. It didn't save Buckingham though, as he was assassinated in 1628.

Three months after his accession to the throne, Charles married Henrietta Maria, the 16-year-old sister of the French monarch Louis XIII: at first the marriage was difficult but after Buckingham's death, the pair were reconciled, fell in love and remained devoted to each other. But marriage to a French princess did not prevent war. When Charles attempted to regain lands seized by Spain from the Elector Palatine, in 1627 England was at war with France. Campaigns foundered and parliament refused its support, so Charles retaliated by dissolving parliament again in 1629. He ruled alone until 1640, a period of personal rule that became known as the 'Eleven Years' Tyranny'. To add to his woes, the imposition of a new prayer book in Scotland raised dissent which soon descended into all-out war.

In what became called the Bishops' Wars of 1639 and 1640, Charles was defeated by the Scots: Charles called on the dissolved parliament to fund his campaigns, but having been ignored for 11 years, parliament would not concede to the king in what they believe were pro-Catholic policies and they further demanded that in future parliament could not be dismissed without its own consent. As arguments raged, dissent grew, and in 1642, when Charles attempted to have five leading dissenters arrested during a visit to the Houses of Parliament, opposition grew into outrage and relations between monarch and the Commons disintegrated.

On 22 August 1642 Charles raised his standard at Nottingham and established his government at Oxford. The Royalists controlled the Midlands, Wales, the west country and the north, while Parliament controlled London and the south-east, as well as East Anglia. The English Civil War began with the Battle of Edgehill on 26 October 1642, and skirmishes continued until the Battle of Naseby was a victory for the well-drilled New Model Army of 'Roundheads' formed by Oliver Cromwell and led by Thomas Fairfax in 1645.

CHARLES I   1625–49

Posthumous title: *Charles, King and Martyr*

Dynasty: *House of Stuart*

Born: *Dunfermline Palace, Scotland on 19 November 1600*

Succeeded to Throne: *27 March 1625*

Crowned at: *Westminster Abbey on 2 February 1626*

Died: *Whitehall, London on 30 January 1649*

Buried: *t. George's Chapel, Windsor Castle, Berkshire*

Authority: *King of Great Britain and Ireland, Virginia, New England, Maryland (from 1632), Nova Scotia (1628–32), Bermuda, and five Caribbean islands.*

Parents: *James I (James VI of Scotland) and Anne of Denmark, their second son and fourth child.*

Married: *Henrietta Maria (1609–69), sister of King Louis XIII of France on 1 May 1625 by proxy at Notre Dame Cathedral, Paris and on 13 June 1625 at Canterbury Cathedral, Kent.*

Children: *Nine, notably Charles II, Henrietta (1644–70), Mary (1631–60) and James II.*

*Catholic Henrietta Maria was the queen of
Charles I and sister of the French king, Louis XIII.*

1625–49

In 1649 Charles was captured and put on trial for high treason, but he refused to acknowledge the legitimacy of the court, staying firm to his belief in the divine right of kings. The massed ranks of judges at Westminster Hall found him guilty of waging war against the country and condemned him to death.

The 'Martyr King' was executed at Whitehall on 30 January 1649 and was buried without ceremony at St. Georges Chapel, Windsor. He apparently wore two shirts for his execution, to prevent any shivers from the cold being seen as a sign of fear or weakness. Henrietta Maria returned to France where she lived until her death in 1669, and their son Charles spent the next 11 years in exile., while England was governed by the Lord Protector, Oliver Cromwell.

The execution of Charles I took place on 30 January 1649. His head was later sewn back onto his corpse before burial.

CHARLES II

1660–1685

While Charles II technically succeeded his executed father in 1649, he would not be crowned and would not rule until 1660. During the Civil War, Charles was sent abroad to safety in Holland, where his sister Mary and her husband William of Orange provided material support for the English royalist cause. In 1650 Charles allied with the Scots launched his attempt to restore the monarchy. He was defeated by Cromwell at the Battle of Worcester, where, according to legend, he hid in an oak tree while fleeing from the battle.

When Oliver Cromwell died in 1658, he was succeeded by his son Richard, but he lacked the power base of his father and was forced to resign as Lord Protector, in 1659. The following year Charles was invited back to England and was crowned king. Once king, Charles divided his attentions between diplomacy and personal pleasure. In 1662, Charles married Catherine of Braganza to cement an anti-Spain alliance with Portugal. (Catherine had buck teeth but did come with a dowry that included Tangiers and Bombay). However, the new king kept a string of mistresses – sometimes two at a time – throughout his life, who bore him some 13 illegitimate children. The most famous were Barbara Villiers and the orange-seller turned actress, Nell Gwynne, who was also popular with the people. When her coach was surrounded by an angry mob who mistook her for the Catholic Duchess of Portsmouth, another of Charles's mistresses, Nell reputedly stuck her head out of the window and said, 'Pray good people be silent. I am the Protestant whore'. One beauty who did not succumb to the royal charms was Frances Stewart, who instead became the model for the figure of Britannia struck on the newly-minted coinage of the Restoration.

While 'Old Rowley's' (the nick named was derived from one of the stallions in the royal stud) private life caused consternation, after the rigorous Puritanism of the Commonwealth, it was also a welcome and largely popular relief. Charles also took a great interest in the arts and sciences: he supported Christopher Wren, established the Royal Observatory at Greenwich and backed the foundation of the Royal Society which became the world's foremost scientific forum. Scientific enquiry and learning flourished, with Isaac Newton, his rival Robert Hooke, and Robert Boyle all making significant contributions to the 'natural sciences'. Literature revived after the Puritan suppression: Milton's *Paradise Lost* and Bunyan's *Pilgrim's Progress* were written during Charles's reign; John Dryden was poet laureate in 1668; and after a long period of closure, the theatres reopened and Restoration comedy came into its own. The Fire of London in 1666 provided the opportunity for the city to be

CHARLES II   1660–1685

Nicknames: *Old Rowley, the Merry Monarch*
Dynasty: *House of Stuart*
Born: *St. James's Palace, London on*
29 May 1630
Succeeded to Throne:
30 January 1649; restored to the
throne on 30 January 1630
Crowned at: *Westminster Abbey*
on 23 April 1661
Died: *Whitehall Palace on 6 February 1685*
Buried: *Henry VII''s Chapel, Westminster*
Abbey
Authority: *King of Great Britain and Ireland,*
ten American colonies, Bombay

(1661–68), Tangier (1662–84),
seven Caribbean islands including
Jamaica (from 1655), Bermuda,
and Gold Coast, Africa.
Parents: *Charles I and Henrietta Maria, their*
eldest surviving son.
Married: *Catherine of Braganza*
(1638–1675) daughter of John IV,
Duke of Braganza and King of
Portugal, on 21 May 1662 at
Portsmouth,
Children: *No legitimate heirs. At least 13*
illegitimate children, including James,
Duke of Monmouth (1649–85),

Nell Gwynne (1650–87) was an actress when she caught the king's eye in 1668. She gave birth to a son, Charles in 1670, who became the first Duke of St Albans, and from 1671 until her death lived in a crown property in Pall Mall.

John Milton was a Puritan, who was arrested at the Restoration for his polemical views. His epic poem Paradise Lost reflects some of the controversies of his day, as well as the sweeping religious themes for which it is famous.

rebuilt, and Sir Christopher Wren transformed London into an elegant, Baroque city. A keen sportsman, Charles also introduced yachting from Holland and in 1661 the world's first yacht race was held when Charles raced his brother James down the Thames.

But the restoration of the monarchy did not come without serious political implications. Religious tensions certainly did not disappear entirely, and foreign policy was to be largely dominated by wars with the Dutch – the first of which coincided with two great 'natural disasters', the Great Plague in 1665 and the Fire of London in 1666. The Treaty of Westminster with the Dutch ceded the Dutch colony New Amsterdam to the British, which was renamed New York in honour of Charles's brother, the Duke of York, as well as New Jersey, so the British now had a string of colonies down the north-east coast of America. In 1670, Charles granted a charter to the Hudson's Bay Company to trade in North America, and this was the beginning of the extremely lucrative fur trade in Canada. In India, the British East India Company was granted the right to acquire land, mint money and command troops on behalf of the crown, laying the foundations of British rule in India.

The Popish Plot revealed by Titus Oates, in 1678 was a supposed plot to murder Charles and restore Catholicism to England. Although the plot was fabricated, it did lead parliament to try to exclude the king's brother, the openly Catholic James Duke of York, from the line of succession. The discovery in 1683 of a real conspiracy, the Rye House Plot to murder both the king and his brother James implicated several Whig politicians who were later executed.

During his final years, the 'Merry Monarch's' income was so great from a booming economy that he had no need to summon parliament again. In 1685 he suffered a stroke and apologised to his doctors for being 'such an unconscionable time a-dying'. Charles sent for a Catholic priest to give him the last rites and before falling into a coma is reputed to have said, 'Let not poor Nelly [Nell Gwynne] starve'.

Charles II was a pragmatic, diplomatic ruler, whose own character fitted the mood of the age perfectly. Tired of Puritanism, the English were ready to welcome a monarch who, in the words of the writer and diarist John Evelyn, was 'a prince of many virtues and many great imperfections, debonair, easy of access, not bloody or cruel'.

JAMES II (JAMES VII OF SCOTLAND)

1685–1688

The brother of Charles II, James, Duke of York had escaped imprisonment by the Parliamentarians in 1648 and fled England for Holland disguised as a girl. He succeeded to the throne in 1685 after his brother Charles II had died without a legitimate heir. As Lord High Admiral during his brother's reign James played a leading role in the naval wars against the Dutch and had his own 'court' at St James Palace which kept him and his wife Anne Hyde in permanent debt (while she grew enormously plump). Like his brother, James was fond of sports, especially hunting and horse racing, but was even fonder of women.

James had spent a large part of his exile in France, which drew him to the Catholic faith of his mother, although Charles II had made sure his brother's daughters Mary and Anne, potential heirs to the throne, were raised as Protestants. When Anne died, in 1673 James married again. His second wife was the Italian – and devoutly Catholic – Mary of Modena, aged only 15 years old (only four years older than his daughter Mary).

James's accession as king took place smoothly, but within months he faced rebellion from the eldest of his brother's illegitimate children, James Duke of Monmouth. Monmouth's rebellion was defeated and retribution handed out to his supporters at the Bloody Assizes.

In 1687 James took the step that would ultimately lead to his downfall: he issued the Declaration of Indulgence aiming at complete toleration for Catholics, Anglicans and Protestants alike, but it was interpreted as a means of restoring Catholicism to England. Anglicans were alarmed and through the Dutch ambassador in London, William of Orange, the Protestant husband of James's daughter Mary began to take sounding of public opinion. A second Declaration was issued in 1688 and the Archbishop of Canterbury and six bishops were put on trial for refusing to read it out in church. There was great rejoicing in the streets when the clergymen were acquitted.

But Protestant suspicions of a 'return to Rome' were further deepened in 1688 when Mary of Modena gave birth to a son, James (who according to Protestant propaganda was not a royal child but one smuggled into Mary's bed in chamber in a warming pan. The boy James would later be known as the 'Old Pretender'). There was now a Catholic heir to the throne. Bishop Compton of London, along with the dukes of Devonshire and Shrewsbury, sent an invitation to William of Orange, assuring him of widespread support should he wish to claim the crown and the 'Glorious Revolution' was begun. In January 1689 parliament formally declared that James II had abdicated: he had fled to France where he plotted his return to power. Still recognised as king in Ireland, on 1 July 1690, he led his army into action at the Battle of the Boyne but was defeated by William's troops. James returned to France where he lived at the chateau of St Germain en Laye, thanks to his cousin Louis XIV, and died in 1701.

JAMES II   1685–1688
(JAMES VII OF SCOTLAND)

Nicknames: *None known*

Dynasty: *House of Stuart*

Born: *St. James's Palace, London on 14 October 1633*

Succeeded to Throne: *6 February 1685*

Crowned at: *Westminster Abbey on 23 April 1685*

Died: *Chateau of Saint Germain-en-Laye, near Versailles on 6 September 1701*

Buried: *Saint Germain parish church and the Church of the English Benedictines, Paris.*

Authority: *King of Great Britain and Ireland, eleven American colonies, seven Caribbean islands and Bermuda.*

Parents: *Charles I and Henrietta Maria, their second son.*

Married:
(1) Anne Hyde (1637–71) daughter of Edward Hyde, Lord Chancellor and 1st earl of Clarendon, on 3 September 1660 at Worcester House, Strand, London, and (2) Maria of Modena (Maria Beatrice d'Este), daughter of Alfonso IV, Duke of Modena on 30 September 1673 by proxy at Modena, and then on 21 November 1673 at Dover, Kent.

Children: *Fifteen, notably Mary II and Anne by (1) and James (the Old Pretender) by (2).*

WILLIAM III   1689–1702

Nicknames: King Billy (posthumous Irish
Protestant salutation)

Dynasty: House of Stuart

Born: The Hague, Netherlands,
on 4 November 1650

Proclaimed King: 13 February 1689

Crowned at: Westminster Abbey
on 11 April 1689

Died: Kensington Palace London
on 8 March 1702

Buried: Westminster Abbey, London

Authority:
King of England, Scotland and Ireland
(respectively as William III, II and I) reigning
jointly with Mary II. Stadholder of the
Netherlands (from 24 June 1672), recognised by
seven American colonies, seven Caribbean
islands, Bermuda, and Dutch overseas
possession.

Parents: Mary (daughter of Charles I) and
Stadholder William II, 4th Prince
of Orange-Nassau)

Married: Mary (Mary II) his cousin and
eldest daughter of the Duke of York
(later James II) on 4 November
1677 at St. James's Palace, London

Children: None

WILLIAM III 1689–1702 MARY II 1689–1694

MARY II   1689–1694

Nicknames: None known
Dynasty: House of Stuart
Born: St. James's Palace, London on 30 April 1662
Proclaimed Queen: 13 February 1689
Crowned at: Westminster Abbey on 11 April 1689
Died: Kensington Palace, London on 28 December 1694

Buried: Henry VII's Chapel, Westminster Abbey
Authority: Queen of England, Scotland and Ireland
Parents: Duke of York (later James II) and Anne Hyde, their eldest surviving daughter
Married: Prince William of Orange (William III) on 4 November 1677 at St. James's Palace, London
Children: None

WILLIAM III & MARY II

WILLIAM III 1689–1702
MARY II 1689–1694

William was James II's nephew and son-in-law: he never knew his father and his mother, Mary Stuart died when he was ten. Short and slight, he grew to be respected but not particularly liked on account of his reserved, abrupt and haughty demeanour. Although he spoke fluent English, he did so with a pronounced Dutch accent. He married his cousin Mary, the daughter of James, then Duke of York. She had the senior claim to the crown, but resigned her rights so that both she and William reigned jointly until her death from smallpox, after which he ruled alone.

William's reason for invading England was to 'rescue the religion and the nation' from Catholicism: he had already fought off Louis XIV's France and the possibility of an Anglo-French alliance appalled him. In 1688 William was expecting a French attack and used the Dutch naval and military preparations as a 'cover' for his invasion of England. In November 1688 William's fleet arrived in Torbay and the following year he and Mary were crowned at Westminster Abbey. In 1689 the Toleration Act guaranteed freedom of worship for all Protestant dissenters, while the First Mutiny Bill outlawed a standing army without Parliament's approval. By this time it was clear that the royal couple would not have children: in the first year of their marriage Mary had suffered two miscarriages and she turned her attentions to supporting William and her devotion to religion.

Nevertheless, when William was away at the wars for nearly eight months out of each year, Mary proved an adept and highly popular Queen-in-Council. Mary was queen for just five years but during this time English forces were active in Ireland, Scotland and France. In May 1689 England declared war on France, and although proclaimed queen (and king) in Scotland, Mary and William faced opposition from the Jacobites such as John 'Bonnie Dundee' Graham, a loyal supporter of James VII of Scotland and II of England. James attempted to restore himself to the throne and launched an assault on Londonderry, but was defeated at the Battle of the Boyne in 1690 and forced to return to France.

When Mary died, William ruled alone. In 1697 the Treaty of Ryswick brought to an end the war with France and two years later, in 1701, a major alliance was formed with Austria and Holland (mainly to prevent a union between France and Spain). At home, the Act of Settlement determined the Protestant succession to the British throne. The Act was passed in 1701, the year of James II's death in exile in France; immediately, Louis XIV recognised James's son, James Edward as the 'rightful' king James III. But the Act of Settlement guaranteed the succession by the Protestant head of the House of Hanover in the (very likely) event that William's heir, his sister-in-law Anne, did not produce an heir herself. William died after falling from his horse after it stumbled on a molehill: he broke his collarbone and seemed to be recovering well when pneumonia set in, and he died in 1702. The Jacobites toasted the mole as 'the little gentleman in black velvet'.

Luois XIV - the 'Sun King' of France.
William's decision to invade England
was partly due to his determination
to avooid an Anglo-French alliance.

ANNE   1702–1714

Nicknames: None known
Dynasty: House of Stuart
Born: St. James's Palace,
    London on 6 February 1665
Succeeded to Throne: 8 March 1702
Crowned at: Westminster Abbey
        on 23 April 1702
Died: Kensington Palace,
    London on 1 August 1714
Buried: Henry VII's Chapel, Westminster Abbey

Authority: Queen of Great Britain and
    Ireland, 12 American colonies,
    seven Caribbean islands, Gibraltar
    (from 1704), Minorca (from
    1708), Nova Scotia (from 1710),
    New Brunswick (from 1713).
Parents: Duke of York (later James II) and
    Anne Hyde, their second daughter
Married: Prince George of Denmark
    (1653–1708), second son of King
    Frederick III of Denmark on 28 July
    1683 at Chapel Royal, St. James's
    Palace.
Children: None surviving her,
    but 17 including miscarriages.

1702–1714

The last Stuart monarch, Anne succeeded her brother-in-law William III in 1702. The younger daughter of James II, she had married Prince George of Denmark in 1683, but the marriage had produced no surviving children. Despite giving birth to 17 children, only one, William Duke of Gloucester, survived longer than a few months, and even he died at the age of 11 in 1700.

Anne inherited a troubled relationship with France, centred on the dispute over the vacant throne of Spain. This developed into the War of the Spanish Succession in 1702. It was this conflict that pitted France, Spain and Bavaria against the British (with allies Austria, the Netherlands, Portugal and Denmark). Under the leadership of John Churchill, Duke of Marlborough, British forces won four major battles – at Blenheim in 1704, Ramillies in 1706, Oudenarde in 1708, and, at Malplaquet in 1709 – which established Britain as a major European power and brought with them new possessions such as Gibraltar and Minorca.

Prince George of Denmark died in 1708. Although he had few accomplishments (Charles II stated that he had, 'Tried him drunk and tried him sober, and there is nothing to him'), Anne was devoted to him and nursed him on his deathbed in spite of the fact that she herself was a virtual invalid, worn out by her 17 unsuccessful pregnancies. For a period, Anne had found consolation in her friendship with Sarah Jennings, a childhood friend, who married John Churchill, later the Duke of Marlborough. The Marlboroughs' advancement was very much bound up with their relationship with Anne, and Sarah seemed to dominate. In 1691 she suggested that she and the queen correspond with each other under the names of Mrs Morley (Anne) and Mrs Freeman (Sarah) to demonstrate the 'equality' of their relationship. Queen Anne rewarded the Marlboroughs with the royal estate at Woodstock near Oxford, where Blenheim Palace was erected, partly as gratitude to the duke for his military successes. A devout Protestant, Anne favoured the Tories, who she regarded as the party of the Church. Sarah favoured the rival Whig faction who pressed for commercial and industrial development and religious toleration. Sarah's unceasing haranguing of the Queen in political matters caused a rift that was never settled.

The later years of Anne's reign saw the introduction of horse racing at Ascot (1711) and the last executions for witchcraft (1712), as well as the Treaty of Utrecht (1713). Signed by Britain and France, the treaty ended the War of Spanish Succession. But the major event of Anne's reign was the Act of Union, the formal creation of the United Kingdom of Great Britain. Placed on the statute books on 6 March 1707, the Act of Union of England and Scotland disbanded Scotland's parliament, although it did leaved unchanged Scotland's legal and ecclesiastical systems. The Act also changed the sovereign's title: Queen Anne was the first Queen of Great Britain and Ireland. Anne died childless, aged just 49 in 1714. The same year the Electress Sophia of Hanover died: her son George became the heir to the English throne and the first Hanoverian king of Britain.

THE HOUSE OF HANOVER 1714–1901

The Act of Settlement passed in 1701 formalised the succession the throne of Britain to exclude all Catholics, which was why James Stuart, 'the Old Pretender', who was the legitimate son of James II was not allowed to reign. At the time the act was concluded, the nearest living Protestant relative was Sophia, Electress of Hanover whose mother was the eldest daughter of James I. Sophia died six weeks before Queen Anne in the summer of 1714 and the succession passed to her eldest son George.

COLONIAL EXPANSION

In the near 200-year rule of the House of Hanover, Britain would see the end of its first empire – the loss of the American colonies after the American War of Independence (1775–83) – and the end of the slave trade. But it would also see the beginnings of the second empire: in 1765 Robert Clive captured Bengal for the East India Trading Company and from then on, Britain extended its rule across India. In 1770 Australia was discovered and the first settlers arrived in the first fleet in 1788, 800 of whom were convicts sent to the new penal colony. The Napoleonic Wars would also bring Britain further colonial possessions, including former French holdings in the Caribbean as well as Malta, the Cape Colony and Ceylon (Sri Lanka). By the mid-19th century British rule extended to much of Africa making it the most powerful colonial power, and 'the workshop of the world', the world's leading trading nation.

INDUSTRIAL REVOLUTION

The centuries of Hanoverian rule in Britain were times of change both for good and bad. The Industrial Revolution, and the concurrent revolution in agriculture began in the mid-18th century and changed the face of the country: land reclamation along with enclosure of the land altered the landscape of Britain, and as greater efficiency in farming and livestock breeding brought increased and cheaper food, the population of Britain grew from around 7 million at the start of the 18th century, to around 38 million by the time of Queen Victoria's reign. But the new manner of farming also forced many of the rural poor from their land: the Highland Clearances in Scotland where homesteads were removed to make way for sheep forced many Scots to emigrate to the colonies, while many others moved from the countryside to the new centres of industry and manufacturing in the growing towns and cities of Britain.

1714-1901

SOCIAL REVOLUTION

With the rise of a new middle class of entrepreneurs, industrialists and professionals, the social climate of Britain changed, with the struggling poor left to fend for themselves or rely on the Church and charity for support. The only alternative for poor without work was the workhouse. It was not until the mid 19th century that a reforming parliament took steps to protect many of the new industrial poor, permitting the establishment of trades unions and in 1847, introducing child labour laws that required children to be over the age of 13 and to work for no more than ten hours a day. It was not until the 1870s that primary education would be compulsory for all children.

THE FIRST PRIME MINISTER

In the reign of Charles II it became the practice for the king to consult a few important ministers in his private apartment or 'cabinet' to discuss affairs of state. By the time of William and Mary, the 'cabinet' of ministers was drawn from the political party with the majority of members of parliament in the House of Commons with one MP nominated as the head. The cabinet oversaw the workings of the government and held weekly meetings with the monarch. The accession of the first Hanoverian king presented a problem: George I spoke only German and could not therefore preside over the cabinet meetings. The issue was solved with the appointment of the First Lord of the Treasury, Robert Walpole, as the prime or first minister of the king from 1721–42. In addition to the appointment, Walpole later received from George II, the town residence and office at 10 Downing Street, which became the official residence of all prime ministers. From the start of the Hanover reign, to the end of Queen Victoria's in 1901, the influence of the monarchy would steadily decline as the power of parliament, the prime minister and the cabinet increased, but the monarchs continued to command respect, loyalty and usually, great popularity.

THE ARTS

The strong industrial and manufacturing base in Britain that made the country and many individuals wealthy also encouraged the arts and sciences to flourish: Handel's *Messiah* (1742) and *Music for the Royal Fireworks* (1748); Daniel Defoe's *Robinson Crusoe* (1719) and Jonathon Swift's *Gulliver's' Travels* (1726); James Boswell's *The Life of Johnson* and Thomas Paine *The Rights of Man* (both 1791); Jane Austen's *Pride and Prejudice* (1813) and Charles Dickens's *Oliver Twist* (1837) are a mere handful of works that demonstrate the scale and diversity of the arts in Britain at the time.

George Washington at the Siege of Yorktown, a decisive battle in the The American War of Independence, 1775–83.

Success in the Napoleonic Wars led to the expanson of the British Empire.

The workhouse: a refuge for the unemployed.

Jane Austen's novels chronicle Regency England.

GEORGE I   1714–1727

Nicknames: None known
Dynasty: House of Hanover
Born: Osnabruck, Hanover, Germany on 28 May 1660
Succeeded to Throne: 1 August 1714
Crowned at: Westminster Abbey on 20 October 1714
Died: Osnabruck, Hanover on 11 January 1727
Buried: Leineschlosskirche, Hanover, reburied at Herrenhausen Palace during the Second World War.

Authority: King of Great Britain and Ireland, twelve American colonies, seven Caribbean islands, Gibraltar, Minorca, New Brunswick, and 2nd Elector of Hanover (from 1698)
Parents: Ernest Augustus (1629–98) 1st Elector of Hanover (1692–98) and Princess Sophia (1630–1714) (granddaughter of James I), their eldest son.
Married: Sophia Dorothea of Celle (1666–1726) a cousin, and daughter of George William, Duke of Luneburg-Celle on 21 November 1682; divorced 1694).
Children: George II and Sophia Dorothea

George I arrived in England to be crowned king at the age of 54, with a limited knowledge and understanding of the country and its people, and speaking not a word of the language. There were over 50 relatives closer in blood to Queen Anne (not least her half-brother Prince James, the 'Old Pretender'), but all were Catholic and thus barred from the English succession. Descended from James I, through his mother Sophia, George was the nearest Protestant claimant to the throne.

George arrived in England in October 1714, and to his credit, spent the majority of his time in the country thereafter. With him came his son George Augustus, Prince of Wales, and his mistresses. George's wife, whom he had married as a beautiful 16-year-old, Sophia Dorothea of Celle was imprisoned in Hanover. After the first few years of marriage, the couple had grown apart and Sophia Dorothea had begun an affair with Philip von Konigsburg, a colonel of the Swedish dragoons. In 1694 George discovered the affair and imprisoned his wife in the Castle of Ahlden, where she remained for the rest of her life. They were divorced in 1694, but Sophia was forbidden to remarry and denied access to her children. The same year Konigsburg disappeared: it was widely believed that George had ordered his death and the Swede's body was said to have been found buried under the floorboards at George's palace in Hanover. Not surprisingly, father and son had a strained relationship – the younger George despised his father for the treatment of his mother – and the Prince of Wales became a focus for political opposition to the king.

George I arrived in London to jeers, not cheers, partly because his personal life was a source of some amusement to the London mob. Many people were also indignant at the imposition of a German as king. He brought with him his long-standing mistress, Ehrengard Melusine von der Schulenburg and their three children, as well as his illegitimate half-sister, Countess Sophia Charlotte von Kielmansegg. The two women were very different physically, Sophia being short and fat, and Ehrengard tall and scrawny. They immediately earned the nicknames ' the elephant and the maypole'. Created Duchess of Kendal in 1719, Melusine may have married George in secret, and Walpole said, 'she was as much the queen of England as anyone was'.

Because of his lack of English (he communicated with his ministers in French), George relied on his close Hanoverian friends and the Whig faction in parliament. Believing that the Tories supported the Jacobites, George was nevertheless suspicious of the strong-minded Robert Walpole, who came to

GEORGE I

1714–1727

dominate politics, and, accustomed to being an absolute monarch in Hanover, struggled to adapt to government via parliament in Britain. However, he played an active part in guiding British foreign policy, helping in the formation of the Triple and Quadruple Alliances against Spain in 1717 and 1718.

In 1715 the Jacobites attempted to put James III on the throne with a rebellion in Scotland. The '15', the first Jacobite rebellion, was a failure, however. The Old Pretender arrived impoverished and late, and failed to win much support. He left and saw out his days in Rome – but left his son, 'Bonnie Prince Charlie' (1720–88) to raise a second rebellion in 1745.

The economic disaster known as the South Sea Bubble in 1720 (when thousands of investors and speculators in the South Sea Company found their investments were worthless) forced George to become reconciled with Walpole. When it was discovered that cabinet ministers and court officials had been involved in the many questionable dealings, Walpole was needed to sort out a national scandal that threatened not only the government, but the Hanover dynasty and to restore order. Walpole was in his element and from then on, wielded enormous power and dominated British politics.

With parliamentary government run efficiently by Walpole, George removed himself further from public affairs and made trips to Hanover in 1720, 1723 and 1726. A reserved man, he disliked being the subject of public curiosity and avoided the royal box at social events. It was while travelling in Germany in 1727 that he suffered a brain haemorrhage and died. Both his son and Walpole were happy to leave him in Germany and George I was buried in Leinschoss Church. His 'Maypole' mistress Melusine retired to Twickenham where, she believed, the late king visited her in the form of a raven.

A diffident man, who was not especially popular with his subjects, George I not only held on to his British realm, but ensured that it was passed on intact to his son George II.

An engraving by William Hogarth satirizes
investors in the South Sea Company.

Charles Edward Stuart, "Bonnie
Prince Charlie" - a thorn in the side
of Hanoverian rulers for many years.

GEORGE II   1727–1760

Nicknames: None known

Dynasty: House of Hanover

Born: Herrenhausen Palace,
Hanover on 30 October 1683

Succeeded to Throne: 11 June 1727

Crowned at: Westminster Abbey
on 11 October 1727

Died: Westminster Palace, London
on 25 October 1760

Buried: Henry VII's Chapel, Westminster Abbey

Authority:
King of Great Britain and Ireland, 13
American colonies (from 1732), Gibraltar,
Minorca (until 1756), parts of the West
Indies, Canada (from 1757), Indian
possessions, in particular Bengal from
1757) and 3rd Elector of Hanover.

Parents: George I and Sophia Dorothea of
Celle

Married: Caroline of Ansbach (1683–1737)
daughter of John Frederick,
Margrave of Brandenburg-Ansbach
on 22 August 1705 at
Hanover, Germany.

Children: Three sons and five daughters,
notably Frederick, Prince of Wales
(1707–51), Anne (1709–59),
William, Duke of Cumberland
(1721–65), Mary (1723–72) and
Louisa (1724–51)

1727-1760

More popular than his father, George had had more time to come to understand the British people- and they him. Although he spoke with a heavy accent, his personal courage won him admiration but it was largely thanks to his wife Caroline of Ansbach whom he married in 1705 that brought him some degree of popularity. Caroline had refused a marriage offer from the future Holy Roman Emperor because it would have required her to become Catholic, and much was made of this fact, helping the Hanoverians to become more accepted as British monarchs. She also softened some of her husbands more abrasive and annoying habits, but could do little to curb his explosive temper and obsessive passion for the strict rules of etiquette.

Caroline was one of the most influential of the Hanoverian consorts: she could flirt and beguile successfully with politicians (Walpole was closely allied to her saying he had 'the right sow by the ear') and she was an enthusiastic gardener with her lasting legacy the creation of Kensington Gardens and the Serpentine. When Caroline died, George was distraught: it was said he could not play cards until the queen cards had been removed from the pack. He promised his dying wife he would not remarry, so instead took for himself a number of mistresses. Both George and Caroline had a difficult relationship with their children: they disliked intensely their eldest son Frederick Louis and preferred the younger William Augustus. Frederick set up his own court at Leicester House where he was able to indulge his passions for art, botany, gambling and naturally, women and much to his parent's annoyance, became a favourite with London society and the population at large.

When George became king in 1727, England was under the strong political control of Robert Walpole, and for the first 12 years of George II's reign, the prime minister's policies kept Britain at peace. When Caroline died in 1737, however, Walpole's star began to wane. Between them they had managed to keep George out of foreign wars, but by 1739 George's belligerence meant that Britain was at war, first with Spain, and then in 1742 with France in the War of the Austrian Succession. At nearly 60 years old, George II took the opportunity to lead an army into the field at Dettingen on 16 June 1743, the last time a British sovereign would command an army in battle. Also at the battle – but on the other side – was Charles Edward Stuart 'the Young Pretender'. In 1745 in his desire to reclaim the Scottish and English thrones, 'Bonnie Prince Charlie' invaded Scotland and on a wave of popularity brought his Jacobite army as far south as Derby. In patriotic reaction, the National Anthem was sung at Drury Lane in London on 28 September 1745. George sent his second son, William, Duke of Cumberland to meet the Scots who were defeated at Culloden in April 1746. Jacobite rebels who were not slain in battle were taken prisoner and shot, neglected to the point of starvation, or sold as slaves in the American plantations. Clan chiefs were stripped of their authority, and the wearing of tartan and kilts, playing the bagpipes and owning of weapons was outlawed and punishable by death.

GEORGE II

1727-1760

The wars against the French continued, but British success brought the expansion of it colonial territories. Robert Clive, who had won Madras in 1746, went on to win control of Calcutta, Chandernagore and Plassey in 1756–57 from the French to ensure Britain controlled all of India. In Canada, James Wolfe (who had also fought at Dettingen and Culloden) took Quebec in 1759 and expelled the French from Canada. As George's reign drew to an end, the British Empire was expanding across the world.

Despite his last Prime Minister, the Duke of Newcastle, saying that George, now deaf, and blind in one eye, was the 'best…master and best friend that a subject ever had', the British still found it difficult to take the 'foreign' Hanoverians to their hearts. To many it seemed fitting that George II died in a rather undignified fashion: he had a heart attack while seated on the lavatory. He was buried alongside Queen Caroline, the last British monarchs to be interred at Westminster Abbey.

The Culloden memorial cairn was erected in 1881 to commemorate the 1745 battle.

The death of James Wolfe at Quebec in 1759 was an occasion of national mourning an the death of a hero, but there was also rejoicing as it became clear that the French had ben expelled from Canada.

Queen Caroline was one of the most influential British consorts. Cultured, attractive and charming, she was more intelligent than her husband and surrounded herself with writers, scientists and artists.

GEORGE III   1760–1820

Nicknames: *Farmer George*

Dynasty: *House of Hanover*

Born: *Norfolk House, St. James's Square,
London on 4 June 1738*

Succeeded to Throne: *25 October 1760*

Crowned at: *Westminster Abbey
on 22 September 1761*

Died: *Windsor Castle, Berkshire
on 29 January 1820*

Buried: *St. George's Chapel,
Windsor Castle, Berkshire*

Authority:

*King of Great Britain and Ireland; from 1 January 1801,
King of the United Kingdom of Great Britain and Ireland.
Recognised by 13 American colonies until 1776; most of the
West Indies; Canada; Sierra Leone (from 1787); Gambia (re-
settled 1816); New South Wales (Australia) (from 1788);
parts of India; Ceylon (now Sri Lanka) and other islands
(from 1795); Malacca (1795-1818); Java (1811-18); Cape
Colony (from 1806); Gibraltar, Corsica (1794-6); Malta*

*(from 1800); the Ionian Islands (Greece)(from 1814);
Minorca (1763-81); 4th Elector of Hanover (de facto
until 1803); King of Hanover (from 1814).*

Parents: *Frederick Louis, Prince of Wales
(1707–51), and Princess Augusta of
Saxe-Coburg-Gotha (1719–72)*

Married: *Charlotte Sophia of Mecklenburg-
Strelitz (1744–1818), youngest
daughter of Charles Louis Frederick
Duke of Mecklenburg-Strelitz on 8
September 1761 at St. James's
Palace, London*

Children: *Fifteen, notably George IV, Frederick,
Duke of York (1763–1827),
William IV, Edward (1767–1825),
Ernest (1771–1851),
Augustus (1773–1843) and
Adolphus (1774–1850)*

GEORGE III

1760–1820

'Farmer George' the third Hanoverian king was the first of the line to have been born and raised in England. The son of Frederick, Prince of Wales, who died in a cricket accident in 1751, George III succeeded his grandfather in 1760. He spoke fluent English and German, but had no interest in Hanover and never went there. He gained his nickname early in his reign after he became interested in agricultural science that he put into practical use at his farms at Windsor and Richmond where he increased yields ten-fold. He was also a great patron of the arts: he commissioned Gainsborough and Lawrence for portraits and was instrumental in founding the Royal Academy in 1768.

Like his forebears, George III, had an eye for the ladies, at least before his marriage. It is said that in his youth he had fallen in love with Hannah Lightfoot, a cobbler's daughter from Wapping and that they secretly married and had three children. He was later attracted to the beautiful Lady Sarah Lennox, but was told it was his duty to marry a suitable foreign princess. In the end, the bride was the plain German princess, Charlotte of Mecklenburg-Strelitz. They were introduced to each other at 3 pm on 8 September 1761 and were duly married six hours later. Surprisingly, the couple fell in love, and became devoted to each other, calling themselves Mr and Mrs King in private. George never took a mistress, and their first son and heir, another George, was born within a year of their marriage, to be followed by a further 14 children. The epitome of respectable and pious living, George was a frugal eater and drinker who disapproved of gambling, while Charlotte relished domesticity. In 1762 George bought Buckingham House (the future Buckingham Palace) and called it the 'Queen's House' and most of their children were born there. George also rebuilt the palace at Kew and Charlotte had a pavilion constructed in the grounds of the Botanical Gardens from which guests could view her menagerie of exotic animals housed in a 3-acre paddock.

While traditional courtiers found life at the royal court dull, the family's lifestyle endeared them greatly to the British people. George had an ideal of kingship and saw himself as the 'patriot king' who would override party political factions and – much to the dismay of politicians – would actively rule in the nation's interests. The British political system was partisan, riven by feuds, and controlled by patronage. George was instinctively a Tory, believing that the Whigs had eroded the power of the monarchy during the reigns of his predecessors. He welcomed Lord Bute as prime minister in 1762, but he was a poor administrator and being of Scottish descent, had Jacobite sympathies. In 1763, popular opinion against him grew and he was forced to resign. A succession of administrations came and went until the Tory Lord North became prime minister in 1770. He met with royal approval and George interfered less with the government. North's tenure was dominated by the revolt of the 13 colonies in America, and it was the final British defeat at Yorktown in 1781 that forced his resignation the following year. During these years, George was a model constitutional monarch, always deferring to the advice of his cabinet. In December 1783, William Pitt the Younger (aged just 24) accepted the king's invitation to form a government and remained in power until 1806.

GEORGE III

1760–1820

The king's constant expression of 'What? What?' was at first taken as a sign of nervousness, but in 1788, it became clear that the king was suffering from an incapacitating disease that made him appear to be mad. In 1788 he was seen talking to a tree in Windsor Great park under the impression it was the King of Prussia and developed an uncharacteristic obscene and lustful passion for the Countess of Pembroke. In fact, George suffered from porphyria, a disease that was neither diagnosed nor properly understood. Constrained in a strait jacket or confining chair, his head blistered to draw out malignant 'humours' from the brain, the king was kept out of the public eye, while opponents called for his eldest son to be made regent.

To the delight of the public (and the queen) the king recovered and went to Weymouth to swim, sail and recuperate. Both he and Prime Minister Pitt enjoyed unprecedented popularity at this time. In 1800 he survived an assassination attempt at Drury Lane Theatre when two shots were fired at him: George ordered the performance to continue and to demonstrate his ease, fell, or at least appeared to fall, asleep.

In 1800 the Act of Union led to the creation of the United Kingdom – that now included Ireland – but the king refused to allow Catholic emancipation, and Pitt resigned over this issue, his popularity further dented by the rigours of the Napoleonic Wars. When bouts of madness recurred in 1801 and 1804, it was clear the king was in no fit state to rule and he was increasingly aggravated by the affairs of his children, in particular by the marital troubles of the Prince and Princess of Wales.

In 1810 a final and severe bout of madness, brought on by the death of his youngest and favourite daughter Amelia, left the king blind and growing increasingly deaf. Although he had lucid moments, George III never fully recovered, and his son George, Prince of Wales was appointed Regent with powers of sovereignty from 5 February 1811. George was confined to Windsor, where he remained until his death in 1820.

William Pitt the Younger became the youngest Prime Minister in history at age 24.

A King George III penny.

*The Royal Family of England in 1787.
Engraving by P. Roberts. King George and
Queen Charlotte are surrounded by their
13 surviving children.*

GEORGE IV   1820–1830

Nicknames: Prinny; the first gentleman of England

Dynasty: House of Hanover

Born: St. James's Palace, London on 12 August 1762

Succeeded to Throne: 29 January 1820

Crowned at: Westminster Abbey on 19 July 1821

Died: Windsor Castle, Berkshire on 26 June 1830

Buried: St. George's Chapel, Windsor Castle, Berkshire

Authority:
King of the United Kingdom of Great Britain and Ireland; Canada; four Australian colonies; most of the West Indies; parts of India; Ceylon (Sri Lanka) and other islands; Malta; Gibraltar; Ionian Islands (Greece); four West African colonies; two South African colonies, and King of Hanover

Parents: George III and Queen Charlotte, their eldest son

Married:
(1) in secret and later annulled, to the Catholic, Mrs Maria Fitzherbert (née Smythe) (1756–1837) on 15 December 1785 at Park Street, Mayfair, London; and
(2) Caroline (1768–1821) his first cousin, the second daughter of Charles, Duke of Brunswick, on 8 April 1795 at the Chapel Royal, St. James's Palace, London

Children: Charlotte (by 2)

1820–1830

Having spent nine years as regent for his incapacitated father George III, George IV acceded to the throne in 1820 and while his reign was notable for the granting of political rights to Catholics, it was his time as 'Prinny' or Prince Regent from 1811 to 1820 for which he is most famous. He was a generous patron of the arts, spending lavishly on the Royal Pavilion at Brighton, which was completely rebuilt in a mock-Oriental style by John Nash. Nash also redesigned much of central London (notably the area around Regent Street and Regent's Park). When he was king, George commissioned Sir Jeffry Wyatville to remodel Windsor Castle, which gained the silhouette it is famous for today. He helped found the National Gallery and he visited Ireland and Scotland – the first Hanoverian to do so.

On his trip north of the border, organized by Sir Walter Scot in 1822, George wore tartan and helped to inspire a new 'romantic' view of the Highlands and islands. His private life was punctuated by affairs: at 16 his first conquest was the actress Mary 'Perdita' Robinson who George had seen perform in Shakespeare's *The Winter's Tale* in 1779 and to whom he wrote love letters under the name of Florizel. Two years later, when George fell for another woman, 'Perdita' was quick to exploit her position: she threatened to make public the letters and Prinny's father had to buy her off. Over the next six years Prinny had a succession of a least a dozen mistresses all of whom cost him or his father a small fortune. Then, in 1785, he met a young widow, Maria FitzHerbert who became the love of his life. George knew he could not officially marry her: she was a widow (twice over), a commoner, and worse, a Roman Catholic. Under the 1701 Act of Settlement marriage to Mrs FitzHerbert would have effectively barred George form becoming king, but his father had also introduced the Royal Marriages Act in 1772 which made any marriages by members of the royal family aged under 25 void unless it had received formal approval from the king and the Privy Council. Undeterred, in 1785 George contracted a secret marriage to Mrs FitzHerbert in the drawing room of her house in Mayfair. Despite his proclamations of undying love, George continued to have many affairs, the most torrid of which was with the Countess of Jersey. He continued to spend lavishly, refurbishing his London residence at Carlton House in Pall Mall.

His disparate lifestyle made him grow so fat he was nicknamed the 'Prince of Whales', and by 1794 he was £600,000 in debt – the equivalent of about £40 million today. His father refused to bail him out and the only way to diminish the debts was for George was to make a legal marriage, produce an heir and win parliament's approval, which would then pay off his debts. When the proposition of marriage to his cousin Princess Caroline of Brunswick was put to him, the prince shrugged and is reputed to have said that, 'one damned German frau was as good as another'. He rudely sent his mistress the Countess of Jersey to meet the bride-to-be on her arrival in England in 1795. Caroline, it turned out, swore like a trooper and refused to wash. The fastidious prince took one look at her and demanded a glass of brandy. Their wedding night passed off without incident: the drunken

GEORGE IV

1820–1830

George fell asleep in front of the fire and only made it to the nuptial bed the next morning. Surprisingly, nine months later a daughter was born, but that would be the only child of the marriage: three days after daughter Charlotte's birth, George made his will leaving one shilling to Caroline and declared that his true wife was Mrs FitzHerbert. The couple separated and Caroline went to live in Blackheath where it was said she took lovers and had one illegitimate child, although an official inquiry, the 'Delicate Investigation', in 1806 found no proof of the claims.

When he became Regent in 1811, he distinguished himself by failing to support the bill for Catholic Emancipation, which would have removed all constraints on Catholics in public office. His influence on politics was limited, but his refusal to appoint a Whig government doomed two Tory ministries to failure as they were forced to share power with the Whigs. None of this political in-fighting helped the prosecution of the war with France.

When George III finally died in 1820, his son was crowned with immense pomp in a ceremony that cost an incredible £243,000 (as compared to £10,000 for George III in 1761). His estranged, but very popular, wife returned and attempted to enter the abbey to be crowned, but on George's orders the doors had been locked against her and she evidently went from door to door hammering and shouting in vain to be let in. Much to her husband's relief, Caroline died only a month later.

As a result of his dissolute living as a youth, George's heath suffered and he became immensely fat. He spent his last years as a virtual recluse at Windsor, gorging on huge quantities of food and barrels of cherry brandy laced with laudanum until he was finally killed by a ruptured blood vessel in his stomach in 1830.

George IV is probably best remembered as an arbiter of good taste and fashion. He was undoubtedly an intelligent and witty man, but was spoiled, lazy and debauched, and inspired little respect among his ministers. George's only daughter Princess Charlotte (and the only legitimate heir from George III's seven sons) had died in childbirth in 1817, prompting the Prince Regent's brothers to rush to the altar in an attempt to produce an heir for the next generation. George IV was succeeded by his brother William, Duke of Clarence.

The coronation of George IV, 1821.

The amazing 'Indian Gothic' style of the Royal Pavilion, Brighton was designed by John Nash.

WILLIAM IV 1830–1837

Nicknames: The Sailor King;
The Royal Tar; Silly Billy

Dynasty: House of Hanover

Born: Buckingham Palace on 21 August 1765

Succeeded to Throne: 26 June 1830

Crowned at: Westminster Abbey
on 8 September 1831

Died: Windsor Castle, Berkshire

Buried: St. George's Chapel,
Windsor Castle, Berkshire

Authority: King of the United Kingdom of Great
Britain and Ireland, and other
possessions as his predecessor George
IV, plus South Australia (in 1836) and
King of Hanover.

Parents: George III and Charlotte of
Mecklenburg-Strelitz, their third son

Married: Princess Adelaide of Saxe-Meiningen
(1792–1849), eldest daughter of
George, 6th Duke of Saxe-
Meiningen, on 11 July 1818 at Kew,
Surrey

Children: Two daughters (died in infancy);
ten illegitimate children by his
mistress, actress Mrs Dorothea
Jordan (1762–1816).

1830-1837

Had George IV's daughter Charlotte not died in childbirth 1817, she would have been queen. Instead, George III's third son William, Duke of Clarence became King William IV in 1830 at the age of 64, and during a period of great political upheaval, proved to be an effective ruler – largely because he was willing to accept the advice of competent ministers.

The general election in 1831 brought a Whig government to power: led by Lord Grey, the Whigs were determined to redistribute parliamentary seats on a more equitable basis by extending the franchise and giving a further half a million men in Britain the right to vote. Fearing the expansion of the new middle class, the House of Lords blocked the reform repeatedly, but William was annoyed by their intransigence. He even agreed to Lord Grey's suggestion that the king appoint sufficient new Whig peers to force the measure through the Tory-dominated House of Lords. William persuaded the Tories that they should not force him to do this, and in so doing, he succeeded in advancing democratic government in Britain. In 1832 the First Reform Act was finally passed and it was now clear that the Crown and the Lords could no longer prevail over the will of the House of Commons.

Known as 'Silly Billy' on account of his often-excitable character that led him to be tactless at times, William had spent his early life in the navy – hence his other sobriquets of 'Royal Tar' and 'Sailor King'. He entered service at 13 as a midshipman and rose through the ranks to command in 1786, his own vessel. In 1790 he retired from active service and settled in Bushey Park with his mistress, the actress Dorothea Jordan who bore him 10 illegitimate children.

In 1811 financial burdens forced him to leave the relationship and search for a wife, although he continued to support his children. The search took seven years and in 1818 he married Princess Adelaide of Saxe-Meiningen. He was 52, and Adelaide was 25. She brought no riches but she did have a kind heart and promised to cherish his illegitimate 'FitzClarence' children (whose mother had since died) and bore him children of their own (although the longest surviving child lived only four months). When he came to the throne, on the basis of his family history and his own 'track record' so to speak, few expected William to be any different from his late brother George IV, but his blunt speech, open manner, sense of duty and lack of extravagance – he insisted that the costs for his coronation should be just one tenth that of his brother's – endeared him the nation.

William seemed to regard himself as a 'caretaker monarch', holding the throne for his niece Victoria and determined to hang on long enough to avoid her mother, the Duchess of Kent (who had snubbed Adelaide and grandly kept her daughter away from the 'royal bastards'), becoming Regent. William succeeded: he reigned for seven years and died of pneumonia and cirrhosis of the liver only weeks after Victoria's 18th birthday. In typical bluntness, his last words to his devoted wife Adelaide at his bedside were 'Bear up! Oh come – bear up, bear up!'

VICTORIA

1837–1901

'I will be good', were the words of the young Victoria when during the reign of William IV, she was shown a genealogical chart indicating how close she was to ascending the throne. The high living and low morals of George IV and his brothers had done little to advance respect for the House of Hanover and William had been a reluctant reformer. All this would change under the new queen: when Queen Victoria died at the end of her 63-year long reign in 1901, many in Britain had known no other monarch. While highly regarded for her honesty and her appreciation of the advice and support of her ministers, Victoria also had a stubborn belief in her own good judgement.

Her reign coincided with some of the most profound political, economic, social and artistic changes in recent history, alongside the expansion of British power and influence around the globe. Furthermore, it was under her that the monarchy itself was transformed into the constitutional model that is recognisable today. In 1836 Victoria met her future husband Prince Albert when he came to London: she was besotted by him and on their second meeting in 1839, Victoria asked him to marry her. It was Albert who impressed on Victoria the strong moral values that the era was to become famous for: while Victoria treasured the memory of their love making (that resulted in nine children) Albert regarded sex as a matter of duty rather than pleasure. Albert also believed that the royal family should be an example to all: while their marriage began with Victoria as queen and Albert as her husband and not 'master of the house', she soon began to defer to his judgement and he soon began to press his moral standpoint on the government, knowing full well that any unbecoming conduct would be criticised and admonished by the queen.

Albert was greatly interested in the social conditions of the country and his genuine concern for the welfare of children and workers that he passed on to his wife gave the reform movement a social and political acceptability that had been missing in previous reigns. With royal backing many of the upper classes joined in campaigns for educational, health, and technological reforms. One of the landmark events of Victoria's long reign was the 1851 Great Exhibition held in Hyde Park and housed in Joseph Paxton's Crystal Palace. Organised by Prince Albert, it was showcase for technological and manufacturing advances and for educating the British population about the products they made and the origin of the resources. The exhibition was, on the one hand, a propaganda coup that demonstrated the wealth and power of the Empire, but it also highlighted the poor state of design in Britain. Albert was determined to rectify this and although it was remarked that he was a 'Man of great taste – all of it bad', Albert earmarked the profits from the exhibition for the building of 'The Museum of Manufactures' at South Kensington (now the Victoria and Albert Museum) and the establishment of new schools of design.

VICTORIA 1837–1901

Nicknames: The Grandmother of Europe

Dynasty: House of Hanover

Born: Kensington Palace, London

Succeeded to Throne: 20 June 1837

Crowned at: Westminster Abbey
on 28 June 1838

Died: Osborne, Isle of Wight
on 22 January 1901

Buried: Frogmore, Windsor Home Park,
Berkshire

Authority: Queen of the United Kingdom
of Great Britain and Ireland, and Empress of
India (from 1 May 1876); 208 major colonies
annexed or leased in Africa and Asia including
New Zealand (1840) and Transvaal (1900)

Parents: Edward, Duke of Kent (George III's
fourth son) and Victoria of Saxe-
Coburg (1786–1861) widow of
Prince Emich of Leiningen and
daughter of Francis, Duke of Saxe-
Coburg-Saalfeld.

Married: Prince Albert of Saxe-Coburg-Gotha
(1819–61), a first cousin and son of
Ernest I, 1st Duke of Saxe-Coburg-
Gotha on 10 February 1840 at St
James's Palace, London

Children: Victoria (1840–1901);
Albert (Edward VII);
Alice (1843–78);
Alfred (1844–1900);
Helena (1846–1923);
Louise (1848–1939);
Arthur (1850–1942);
Leopold (1853–84)
and Beatrice (1857–1944)

The Great Exhibition, 1851.

Queen Victoria succeeded to the throne at the age of 18.

The Albert Memorial in London was opened in 1872 and is one of several monuments erected in memory of the Prince Consort.

The Crimean War prompted the award of a new medal for valour – the Victoria Cross.

VICTORIA

In 1861 Albert died, probably of typhoid, and Victoria was grief stricken. She spent the rest of her life in mourning dress, commissioning the Albert Hall and Albert Memorial in his memory. After his death Victoria took a less active role in public affairs, but was kept fully informed by close contact with her many prime ministers. At the beginning of her reign Lord Melbourne, proffered avuncular advice, until he was succeeded by Sir Robert Peel (whose downfall came after he pushed through the Repeal of the Corn Laws in 1846). Lord Palmerston took the country to war in the Crimea from 1854-56. She suffered four terms of office under William Gladstone who, she said, 'addresses me as if I were a public meeting' (and who extended the franchise further in 1884 with the Second Reform Act). Benjamin Disraeli, who made her Empress of India in 1876 and took over the Suez Canal (an important trade route to India).

During her self-imposed withdrawal Victoria sought comfort and companionship from her large family and her friends, notably her Scottish manservant John Brown. Her friendship with Brown and his informal, yet highly protective treatment of her gave rise to rumours that the pair were lovers. She retreated to Osborne House on the Isle of Wight (designed by Albert in a fashionable 'Italianate' style and Balmoral, in the Scottish Highlands (rebuilt, again to Albert's plans, in the 1850s). The public began to grow weary of this extended period of mourning and there were calls for her abdication in favour of the Prince of Wales. Disraeli knew how to deal with the queen: he said, "When it comes to royalty, you should lay it (flattery) on with a trowel" and so encouraged the queen out of mourning. In 1874 she went to balls, toured the country and rode in an open carriage. By the time of her Golden Jubilee in 1887 Victoria had won back the affection and respect of the people and the occasion was marked by celebrations throughout the Empire.

Through the marriages of her nine children and 42 grandchildren, Victoria became related to the royal families of Greece, Sweden, Spain, Germany, Norway, Russia and Romania: she once said she could relax with any European royal because they were all equals, but she did relish the fact that she was the 'Grandmother' of the European royal families. Of her nine children, three predeceased her: Alice in 1878 (the queen's granddaughter, also called Alice, married Tsar Nicholas II); Leopold in 1884, and Alfred in 1900. Her last surviving child, Beatrice died in 1944.

When Queen Victoria died at Osborne House on 22 January 1901, she had reigned longer than any other previous British monarch. Furthermore, she reigned over more people as her subjects than any other: one quarter of the Earth's surface flew the Union Jack. She asked to be buried with two tokens beside her: one of Albert's dressing gowns, and a lock of John Brown's hair alongside a picture of him.

THE HOUSE OF WINDSOR 1901–PRESENT

THE HOUSE OF SAXE-COBURG-GOTHA

Edward VII was Britain's first and only Saxe-Coburg-Gotha sovereign. Sometimes also called the 'House of Wettin', the line took its name from the German duchy of the same name from which Prince Albert, the son of Duke Ernest I of Saxe-Coburg and Gotha, was descended. The name was retained until 1917 when, during World War I, anti-German sentiment in Britain was at its height; in a demonstration of British patriotism (since Kaiser Wilhelm of Germany was his cousin) King George V renamed his dynasty the House of Windsor.

THE END OF AN EMPIRE, THE START OF THE COMMONWEALTH

At the beginning of the century, the British Empire extended its rule to almost one-third of the world's population, but by the 1930s, the Empire began to fracture. In 1931, the Statute of Westminster recognized Australia, Canada, Eire, South Africa and New Zealand as independent states within the Commonwealth of Nations. At the end of World War II, the 'map of the world' was once again redrawn. Former colonial rulers, no longer the formidable powers they had been, withdrew their rule to allow independent nation-states to emerge. India and Pakistan became independent in 1948, as did Burma and Sri Lanka, followed by the establishment of the new state of Israel out for the former British-mandated territory of Palestine. By the end of the 1960s most of the former British colonies in Africa, the Caribbean and the Pacific were also independent and in 1997 Hong Kong was returned to China. By the end of the 20th century, Britain retained 14 overseas territories, such as Gibraltar and the Falkland Islands – and both of these were the subject of dispute by Spain and Argentina respectively. Today, the Commonwealth comprises nearly 50 nations and represents over one billion people on every continent.

The areas coloured red on this map were at different times ruled by Britain.

HOUSE OF WINDSOR

1901–PRESENT

A CENTURY OF CONFLICT

As with all eras, the reign of the Windsors was not without conflict, both at home and abroad. The revolutionary ferment in Russia which had been brewing since 1905 erupted in 1917 and led to the abdication and later execution of Tsar Nicholas II, while in 1916 the Easter Rising in Dublin in support of Irish independence paved the way for a landslide victory for Sinn Fein MPs in Ireland who refused to sit at Westminster and instead formed their own parliament (the Dail) in Dublin in 1918. Two years later, Ireland was partitioned into the Irish Free State and the province of Northern Ireland. The 'Troubles' in the north of Ireland re-surfaced in 1969 and for the next 25 years, the conflict became bloodier and deadlier. In 1936, the Spanish Civil War saw thousands of Britons join the International Brigade to fight with the Republicans against the right wing military leadership General Francisco Franco who was supported by Fascist Italy and Nazi Germany. Two World Wars, the first from 1914–18 and the second, from 1939–45, brought about the deaths of some 10 million people in the first, and over 55 million in the second, and ushered in the atomic age with the dropping of atomic bombs on Hiroshima and Nagasaki. After 1945 the polarisation of power between the United States of America and the Soviet Union escalated into Cold War, which remained tense until the fall of the Berlin Wall and the collapse of the Soviet Eastern Bloc in 1989. In 1956 Anglo-French forces invaded Egypt after the Suez Canal was nationalised and in 1982, Britain went to war with Argentina over control of the Falkland Islands (Las Malvinas) in the South Atlantic Ocean.

A CENTURY OF CHANGE

The 20th century, often called the 'second industrial age', was a century of enormous change: it witnessed the arrival of new telecommunications media, such as the telephone, radio, movies, television and later the electronic and digital media. Air travel, first in dirigibles (air ships or zeppelins), was soon overtaken by fixed wing aircraft (and later helicopters) and then in the post-war period by space exploration. Society in Britain was hugely affected by these advances and likewise saw enormous change take place:. The 1911 National Insurance Act provided sickness and unemployment benefits; women were enfranchised for the first time in 1918 and the following year Lady Astor became the first woman to take her seat as an MP. In 1948 the National Health Service was founded and established free medical treatment for all. Gradually, class distinctions in Britain became blurred and old style deference – even to the monarchy – began to fade. The royal family in the 20th century responded equally to these changes – especially through the use of the media with radio and television broadcasts to the nation and Commonwealth – to create a modern constitutional monarchy which acted a as symbol of the nation, rather than wielding political power and that also shared many of the same trials and tribulations of modern families.

Global conflicts punctuated the 20th century.

Over 50 million people died in World War II.

Suffragettes campaigned for votes for women in the early years of the 20th century.

One of the greatest advances of the 20th century was space exploration.

EDWARD VII   1901-1910

Nicknames: Bertie, Tum-Tum, The Peacemaker

Dynasty: House of Saxe-Coburg-Gotha

Born: Buckingham Palace, London on 9 November 1841

Succeeded to Throne: 22 January 1901

Crowned at: Westminster Abbey on 9 August 1901

Died: Buckingham Palace on 6 May 1910

Buried: St George's Chapel, Windsor Castle, Berkshire

Authority: King of the United Kingdom of Great Britain and Ireland and British Dominions Overseas; Emperor of India

Parents: Queen Victoria and Price Albert of Saxe-Coburg-Gotha

Married: Princess Alexandra of Denmark (1844–1925) daughter of King Christian IX of Denmark, on 10 March 1863 at St George's Chapel, Windsor Castle, Berkshire

Children: Six, including Albert Victor (1864–92), George V, Louise (1867–1931), Victoria (1868–1935) and Maude (1869–1938)

1901–1910

Edward VII can be regarded as either the last Hanoverian monarch, or, the first – and only – Saxe-Coburg-Gotha sovereign: he was a Hanoverian on his mother's (Queen Victoria) side and a Saxe-Coburg-Gotha on his father's (Prince Albert). One aspect that marks him out as a true Hanoverian, is the very difficult relationship he had with his parents. His father, Prince Albert, was constantly upheld by his mother as the model of manhood, but 'Bertie' as he was known in the family, was very different to him and consequently, his parents found him a 'great disappointment'.

When he travelled on a state visit to France in 1854 aged 13, he allegedly told the Emperor Napoleon III, 'I would like to be your son' and from then on, Edward remained pro-French. In 1904 he encouraged the *Entente Cordiale* between Britain and France, a treaty of diplomatic and military co-operation that united the two countries against German aggrandizement.

Although he spoke several languages, he was a poor speller. Furthermore the constant stress placed on him by his parents who thought 'poor Bertie' was slow and 'backwards' caused him to stammer. Bertie was given a household at White Lodge in Richmond Park where three aids were appointed to teach him manners and polite conversation- and to keep him away from billiards and cards. At 19 he was sent to Ireland for military training where his fellow officers slipped a young girl Nellie Clifden, into his bed. Word of the affair leaked out and upset his parents: vengefully Victoria insisted that this had caused such strain as to be the actual cause (and not typhoid) of her beloved Albert's death in 1861.

Two years later Bertie married Princess Alexandra of Denmark and the couple moved to Marlborough House in Pall Mall where they entertained their society friends and where Alexandra devoted her time to charity work and raising their children – and patiently stood by her husband in spite of his many and much publicised affairs. His most famous mistresses included the actress Lillie Langtry and Alice Keppel (whose second daughter, Sonia, was widely believed to be Edward's child. Her granddaughter, Camilla Parker-Bowles, became the Duchess of Cornwall, the second wife of Charles, Prince of Wales).

Two scandals. in particular. required the prince's presence in court, an unprecedented event for royalty in itself. In 1870 he was called to give evidence in the divorce case of Sir Charles and Lady Mordaunt (Edward was cited as one of the co-respondents); and in 1890 an illegal game of baccarat at a house party in Tranby Croft in Yorkshire gave rise to accusations of cheating and an action for slander.

EDWARD VII

1901–1910

During the years of his mother's widowhood, Edward and his wife shouldered many of her royal duties in the queen's place, opening new institutions and appearing on state occasions. The prince was immensely popular, and when he was seriously ill with typhoid in 1871, the nation held its breath. He recovered, and so great was the feeling of relief, that his mother ordered a national service of thanksgiving. Edward spent eight months touring India in 1875, and it was partly because of his diplomacy that the queen was able to assume the title Empress of India in 1876.

The succession to the throne seemed secure, as Edward and Alexandra had five surviving children, but in 1892 tragedy struck with the death of their eldest son, Albert Victor (known as Eddy) from pneumonia. A rather slow young man, Albert Victor was possibly not ideal monarch material, but his death was a heavy blow to his family. 'To lose our eldest son'' he wrote to his mother, 'is one of those calamities one can never really get over'. Their second son, George, Duke of York, stepped seamlessly into his brother's place, even marrying his fiancée, Princess Mary of Teck.

Edward spent most of his adult life 'waiting in the wings': he was 59 when he ascended the throne in 1901 and significantly chose to be crowned as Edward VII and not Albert I. He had all the royal palaces refurbished, destroying any traces of his mother's servant and companion John Brown, and continued to enlarge the house, landscape the gardens and improve the farms on the Sandringham Estate in Norfolk that he had bought in 1862. When not engaged in royal duties Edward continued to enjoy the good life. Horseracing was a passion – his horse Minoru won the Epsom Derby in 1906 – as were hunting, shooting and motoring in the new 'horseless carriages'.

Shortly after his coronation in 1902 he bought a Renault and a Mercedes and had the royal coat of arms added to each of the door panels. His love of France took him often to Monte Carlo, where his patronage helped to make the town into a fashionable resort where he could indulge his passion for cards and fine dining. Even the king's increased girth had an impact on fashion: to accommodate his growing frame, Edward had his tailor devise the Norfolk Jacket for shooting and it became the fashion to leave the bottom button of a waistcoat unfastened in imitation of the king.

Although king for only nine years, and in the latter part in ill health, Edward was an immensely popular monarch whose death was keenly felt at home and abroad. His love of foreign travel and his fondness for the pomp of public ceremonial that established the tradition for the monarch to attend the State Opening of Parliament, also ushered in an 'ambassadorial' style of monarchy that replaced its earlier political role.

Lillie Langtree: the 'Jersey Lily' had an affair with Edward from 1877–80.

Edward VII, an early adopter of the new motorcar technology, with Lord Montague of Beaulieu 1909.

GEORGE V 1910-1936

Nicknames: The Sailor King

Dynasty: House of Saxe-Coburg-Gotha until 17 July 1917 when re-named the House of Windsor

Born: Marlborough House, London on 3 June 1865

Succeeded to Throne: 6 May 1910

Crowned at: Westminster Abbey on 22 June 1911; Coronation Durbar at Delhi, India on 12 December 1911

Died: Sandringham House, Norfolk on 20 January 1936

Buried: St. George's Chapel, Windsor Castle, Berkshire

Authority: King of the United Kingdom of Great Britain and Ireland and British Dominions Overseas; Emperor of India

Parents: Prince Albert Edward (later Edward VII) and Princess Alexandra of Denmark, their second son

Married: Princess Mary of Teck (1867–1953) daughter of Francis, Duke of Teck, on 6 July 1893 at St. James's Palace, London

Children: Edward VIII; George VI; Mary, Princess Royal (1897–1965); Henry, Duke of Gloucester (1900–74); George, Duke of Kent (1902–42); John (1905–19)

1910–1936

George V was the second son of king Edward VII and it was on the death of his older brother Albert Victor, (known as 'Eddy' in the family) in 1892 that he became heir to the throne. Eddy died of pneumonia, but it was later believed he suffered from syphilis of the brain. It was also rumoured that he had secretly married Annie Crook in the mid-1880s and that the infamous 'Jack the Ripper' murders were committed to silence 'those in the know' although there is no evidence to support this.

George joined the navy as a midshipman at the age of 12 and rose to the rank of commander. His love of the sea never left him and he became known as the 'Sailor King' later in life. His brother's death ended his naval career, and George was required not only to assume his place in the line of succession, but also to marry his grief-stricken fiancée, Princess Mary of Teck. The couple married in 1893, and seemed happy and well-suited, producing a family of five sons and a daughter. They lived in the rather cramped surroundings of York Cottage on the Sandringham Estate, where their lifestyle echoed that of the middle classes rather than the aristocracy. Both George and Mary were shy and retiring by nature, the prince preferring nothing more than studying his stamp collection or shooting.

Although George had been instructed in the political processes of parliament, shortly after he became king in 1910 he was embroiled in a crisis: the Liberal government's budget of 1909 had included a new 'super-tax' to cover the costs of an old-age pension, but Lloyd-George's budget was rejected by the House of Lords. In a manner that echoed Lord Grey's request to King William IV in 1831, Prime Minister Asquith had asked Edward VII to consider appointing additional Liberal peers to the House to guarantee the vote's passage on a second reading. Edward had died without making a decision and now George found himself in a difficult position; he made it clear that as a constitutional monarch he should not be drawn into politics. Finally, the matter was sent to committee and a general election was called. When a bigger Liberal majority won the Commons, the Lords were forced to accept that the public had voted for the budget proposals and the social reforms it brought.

Crowned at Westminster Abbey in June 1911, George also decided he should be crowned Emperor in India – something that neither his grandmother, Queen Victoria, nor his father had done. In December 1911 George and Mary were jointly crowned in India's new capital of Delhi. In the years leading up to World War I George had to deal with the possibility of civil war in Ireland after Asquith attempted to introduce the Home Rule Bill, and opponents in Ulster mobilised an armed volunteer resistance. The king called an emergency meeting at Buckingham Palace to consider an amended Home Rule Bill that excluded Ulster, but no decision was reached and the discussions were set aside because on 1 August 1914, George's cousin, Kaiser Wilhelm of Germany declared war on

GEORGE V

1910–1936

Russia and France. To add to the emergency, Germany marched through Belgium to invade France with whom, in 1904, Britain had established the *Entente Cordiale* guaranteeing mutual support and defence.

George did what he could to show his patriotism and to keep morale high, both at home where he and his family shared in the rationing scheme, and abroad, paying several trips to the armies in the field in France and Belgium. When anti-German sentiment became intense, George announced that the family name was to be changed from Saxe-Coburg-Gotha to Windsor.

After the war there was still little peace and the Russian Revolution brought personal tragedy: George's cousin Alice had married Tsar Nicholas II and the couple and their children were killed by Bolshevik revolutionaries in July 1918. In Ireland, support for the nationalists had increased, particularly following the execution of Patrick Pearse and James Connolly who had led the Easter Uprising in April 1916. In 1920 the Government of Ireland Act proposed separate parliaments in Dublin and Belfast and in June 1921 George and Mary opened the Ulster Parliament. By December, the Anglo-Irish Treaty recognized all of Ireland bar Ulster as the Irish Free State.

The end of the decade saw economic decline on a global scale and by the 1930s, Britain was deeply affected by the Great Depression. The king effectively took a pay cut by making cuts to the Civil List and encouraged a National Government to tackle the wider issues of poverty and unemployment: in 1931 this came into power under Ramsay MacDonald. Two other 'reforms' were introduced by George and became part of royal tradition: the distribution of Maundy Money on the Thursday before Easter (a event that dated back to Edward II in 1363 but since the Reformation had been undertaken by the Lord High Almoner) and the Christmas Day radio broadcast.

In 1931 the Statute of Westminster began the change from Empire to Commonwealth: parliament ceased its control over many of Britain's overseas dominions. While George remained head of the Commonwealth, and indeed head of state in some instances, the old imperial world' into which he had been born was disappearing. His health, too, was also in decline: a bout of septicemia in 1928 left him weakened and he had been sent to Bognor Regis to recuperate in the sea air. A lifelong smoker, in 1935 George suffered a severe bronchial infection from which he never really recovered. Queen Mary suggested that he would soon be well enough to visit Bognor again. Apparently, the king's last words before his death in January 1936 at Sandringham, were 'Bugger Bognor!'

George V has been criticised for not doing enough to save his Russian relatives in 1917.

The Depression of the 1930s blighted the last years of George V's reign.

EDWARD VIII

1936

In 1936, not for the first time in its near thousand-year history, the monarchy was in crisis. The Prince of Wales, born Edward Albert Christian George Andrew Patrick David, but known as David to his family and friends, was popular and enjoyed fashionable society, dancing and nightclubs, preferring them to the staidness and pomp and ceremony of royal life. As a young man he had several affairs – one with a married woman, Freda Dudley Ward, another with an American socialite, Thelma, Lady Furness – much to the dismay of his parents, George V and Queen Mary.

Prince Edward had been brought up with the expectation that he would be king, and had been thoroughly tutored for his future. He was invested as Prince of Wales in a ceremony at Caernarvon Castle in 1911, and enlisted in the Grenadier Guards in 1914. Between 1919 and 1925, he embarked on a tour to visit every corner of the British Empire, as well as touring the United States. Edward was thrilled by America – and America was enamoured of him. After his return Edward bought Fort Belvedere, a country house in Virginia Water in Surrey where he kept an informal court. It was here in 1934 that he met his 'true love' Wallis Simpson, who he became determined to marry.

The 'problem' with Wallis was that she was a divorcée – and she was still married to her second husband Ernest Simpson. The prince's relationship alarmed both his family and the government. George V died in January 1936 and Edward became king, believing that he would be able to have his way. In November Prime Minister Stanley Baldwin informed him that his marriage to a twice-divorced woman could not be reconciled with his status as head of the Church of England, but Edward insisted on marriage. Until December 1936, most people in Britain were unaware of the details of the king's relationship with Mrs. Simpson and the ensuing constitutional crisis. Baldwin has requested and received a 'press black-out', although overseas, particularly in America, the situation was common knowledge. The story broke in the British press in December 1936, with reports that the government, the Church of England and the dominions overseas, were opposed to the marriage, although among ordinary people the king had great support. The abdication document was signed at Fort Belvedere and witnessed by his brothers and a financial settlement was arranged for the couple. The following evening, after a farewell dinner with his family, Edward made a broadcast to the nation, explaining that he could not carry on as king 'without the help and support of the woman I love'. His reign had lasted only 325 days.

After the broadcast, Edward, now His Royal Highness the Duke of Windsor, left for France and the following year married Wallis, who was not permitted to style herself as 'Her Royal Highness', something that Edward bitterly resented. When World War II broke out, the duke and duchess fled France for Spain, before being posted to Bermuda as governor. After the war they returned to Paris where they lived for the rest of their lives. The duke died of cancer in 1972; Wallis lived on alone for a further 14 years. Both are buried at Frogmore Mausoleum, Windsor.

EDWARD VIII 1936

Nicknames: None

Dynasty: House of Windsor

Born: White Lodge, Richmond Park, 1894

Succeeded to Throne: 20 January 1936

Crowned at: Never crowned; abdicated 10 December 1936

Died: 28 May 1972, Paris

Buried: Frogmore Mausoleum Windsor, Berkshire

Authority: King of the United Kingdom of Great Britain and Ireland and British Dominions Overseas; Emperor of India

Parents: George, Duke of York (later George V) and Mary of Teck (later Queen Mary), their eldest son

Married: Wallis Warfield Simpson, (1896–1986) on 3 June 1937 at Château de Candé, near Tours, France

Children: None

GEORGE VI 1936–1952

Nicknames: None known

Dynasty: House of Windsor

Born: York Cottage, Sandringham, Norfolk on 14 December 1895

Succeeded to Throne: 11 December 1936

Crowned at: Westminster Abbey on 24 May 1937

Died: Sandringham House, Norfolk on 6 February 1952

Buried: St. George's Chapel, Windsor Castle, Berkshire

Authority: King of the United Kingdom of Great Britain and Northern Ireland and British Dominions Overseas; Emperor of India (until 22 June 1947), Head of the Commonwealth (from 1949)

Parents: George, Duke of York (later George V) and Mary of Teck (later Queen Mary), their second son

Married: Lady Elizabeth Bowes-Lyon (1900–2002), youngest daughter of Claude Bowes-Lyon, 14th Earl of Strathmore and Kinghorne, on 26 April 1923 at Westminster Abbey

Children: Elizabeth II and Margaret (1930–2002)

1936–1952

When his elder brother Edward abdicated the throne in December 1936, the Duke of York had only a week to come to terms with, and prepare, for the fact that he was king. As the second son of George V the new George VI, crowned in May of the following year, and had not expected to rule. Called 'Bertie' in the family, he had been a sickly child who also had a stammer, but he joined the Royal Navy as a cadet at Osborne and Dartmouth naval colleges. When World War I broke out in 1914, George saw active service, notably at the Battle of Jutland, in 1916 before transferring to the Royal Naval Air Reserve and becoming a pilot in 1918 in the newly formed Royal Army Flying Corps (later the Royal Air Force).

After the war ended, George spent a year at university at Cambridge and in 1920 was created Duke of York. It was at this time that George became reacquainted with Lady Elizabeth Bowes-Lyon and the pair married in 1923. Their couple's first child Elizabeth, (later Elizabeth II) was born in 1926, and their second, Princess Margaret in 1930. Content with their family life at home in Bruton Street in London, the Duke and Duchess of York went about their business quietly, working for charities and good causes such as the Duke of York's Boys' Camps which brought together all classes of youngster in outdoor in camping expeditions. The prince was also a fine tennis player- perhaps the best royal player since Henry VIII – and good enough to compete in doubles matches at Wimbledon in 1926. The duchess introduced him to a speech therapist, who helped him to overcome his considerable stammer.

With the death of his father George V and Edward's abdication in 1936, the family were soon thrust into the spotlight. The coronation ceremony in May 1937 was covered by the BBC which broadcast the event worldwide via the radio. In 1939, the king and queen toured Canada and made a brief trip to the USA, where they were met by enthusiastic crowds. Their visit was intended to drum up support for Britain, which would become vital in the event of war with Hitler's Germany. They made a state visit to France in 1938 for similar reasons and with equal success.

With the outbreak of war in September 1939, plans were drawn up for the evacuation of the family to a safe country such as Canada but George and Elizabeth would not hear of it. 'The children won't leave without me. I won't leave without the King – and the King will never leave,' said the queen robustly. Remaining in Britain throughout World War II endeared them to the nation: the king made several trips to visit front line troops stationed abroad (he had wanted to accompany the D-Day landings personally and had to be persuaded not to) and together with his wife visited the devastated East End of London that had been bombed during the Blitz. Despite their royal status, they insisted on imposing rationing on Buckingham Palace, sharing the hardship of the rest

1936–1952

of the nation. In 1940, Buckingham Palace itself was damaged by the Luftwaffe, prompting the queen to say, 'I'm glad we have been bombed. Now I can look the East End in the face'. On the king's initiative, the George Cross and the George Medal was instituted for acts of conspicuous bravery by civilians. In 1942 the George Cross was awarded to the island of Malta, which had suffered relentless bombing by the Germans, but had remained in Allied hands.

When World War II ended, the royal family and Buckingham Palace became the focus of celebration: as crowds gathered on the Mall and outside the palace, to their delight, the king and queen to appeared on the balcony to acknowledge the cheers. Time and time again the royal family were called back to the balcony to wave at the happy revellers.

The return of peace saw the introduction of social changes that the king regarded as great advances: the new Labour government reformed the welfare state and established the National Health Service and introduced reforms to nationalise many British industries.

In the aftermath of the war, India and Pakistan finally won their independence which marked the death of the British empire. Many countries retained their connection to the 'mother country' through the Commonwealth, with George VI as its symbolic head.

The war years had taken their toll on the king's health. Always a heavy smoker, he suffered from arteriosclerosis and was diagnosed with lung cancer. He had his left lung removed in September 1951 and appeared to make a good recovery.

Geroge VI ensured that his elder daughter Princess Elizabeth was well trained for the duties of a monarch, and after her marriage in 1947, she began to take on an increasing number of royal duties. In January 1952, despite medical advice to the contrary, the king waved off Princess Elizabeth and Prince Philip from Heathrow, who were leaving on an extensive tour of the Commonwealth. The king returned to Sandringham, but contracted pneumonia. A week later, having enjoyed a day of shooting, the king was discovered dead by his valet.

As George VI lay in state at Westminster Hall, he was attended by three queens in mourning: his mother Queen Mary, his widow Queen Elizabeth, the Queen Mother as she was now called, and his daughter, the new monarch, Queen Elizabeth II. The funeral tributes included one from the wartime Prime Minister Winston Churchill in the form of the George Cross, which bore the words 'For Gallantry'.

George VI and Queen Elizabeth in London during the Blitz.

Balmoral remains the Scottish retreat of the royal family.

ELIZABETH II 1952–

Nicknames: *None known*

Dynasty: *House of Windsor*

Born: *17 Bruton Street, London on 21 April 1926*

Succeeded to Throne: *6 February 1952*

Crowned at: *Westminster Abbey on 29 May 1953*

Authority: *Queen of the United Kingdom of Great Britain and Northern Ireland and other realms and territories; Head of the Commonwealth and Head of State for 16 of its members.*

Parents: *Duke of York (later George VI) and Lady Elizabeth Bowes-Lyon, later Duchess of York, Queen and on widowhood, HM the Queen Mother)*

Married: *Philip, Duke of Edinburgh (born 10 June 1921), only son of Prince Andrew of Greece and Princess Alice (great-grand daughter of Queen Victoria) on 20 November 1947 at Westminster Abbey*

Children: *Charles, Prince of Wales (b.14 November 1948); Anne, Princess Royal (since 1987) (b. 15 August 1950); Andrew, Duke of York (b. 19 February 1960); Edward, Earl of Wessex (b. 10 March 1964)*

1952–

With her father George VI's accession in 1936, Elizabeth II became heir to the throne at the age of ten and was then carefully prepared for the role to come. Following her coronation, Elizabeth II has become the most photographed, and the most widely travelled monarch in British history – and perhaps the world. As the head of one of a constitutional monarchy, Elizabeth's role is largely formal, although her ceremonial responsibilities to parliament, the armed forces (as monarch she is commander in chief of the entire British armed forces), Church and state have remained largely unchanged.

Until the abdication of her uncle Edward VIII, Elizabeth and her family enjoyed a relatively normal family life at their home in Bruton Street, just off Piccadilly. She was joined in the nursery by her sister Margaret in 1930 and aged seven Elizabeth was pictured in the national press with her Welsh corgi, dogs which have been associated with her ever since. When her father was named king in late 1936, the family was now thrust into the public gaze, with Elizabeth now heir apparent.

Her teenaged years were dominated by the Second World War, and in 1939 she met for the first time, the man who would become her husband. Aged only 13, Elizabeth was on a visit to the Royal Naval College at Dartmouth when she met her third cousin, the 18-year-old Philip of Greece, son of Prince Andrew of Greece. Of Danish descent, Philip was the grandson of King George of the Hellenes and on his mother's side, the great-great-grandson of Queen Victoria. Elizabeth and Philip were married in 1947; on that day Philip was created Duke of Edinburgh and Elizabeth's corgi Susan rode back from the ceremony with the newlyweds in the carriage to Buckingham Palace.

Philip had taken British citizenship and the Mountbatten surname of his mother's family (he was the nephew of Earl Mountbatten) in preference to what was an 'overly-foreign' one. Schleswig-Holstein-Sonderburg-Glucksburg was not only long and difficult to pronounce, but in the post-war years it was considered to have negative connotations. Nevertheless, the wedding lifted the post-war gloom and cheered the nation, whose spirits were lifted further the following year with the birth of the couple's first child, Prince Charles. Three more children followed: Anne, Princess Royal in 1950; Andrew, Duke of York in 1960, and, Edward, Earl of Wessex was born in 1964.

In 1952 Elizabeth and Philip left for a tour of the Commonwealth, but only a week after leaving London, on 6 February, while on safari in Kenya, Elizabeth was told of her father's death in England. Quickly returning to London, the 25-year-old princess assumed her duties as queen and the preparations for her coronation began.

ELIZABETH II

1952–

In addition to her new state role, the Queen immediately had to make decisions concerning the personal lives of her family. Her sister Princess Margaret informed her that she wanted to marry a divorcé, Group Captain Peter Townsend. With the spectre of the abdication still hovering over the monarchy, Townsend was never going to be considered a suitable husband for the princess, and three years later in 1955 the couple split irrevocably. In March 1953, the queen's grandmother the redoubtable Queen Mary died, having given strict instructions that her demise was not to interfere with her granddaughter's coronation.

The coronation of Elizabeth II served to demonstrate the continuity of the British monarchy even though the coronation ceremony itself was modernised a little: while it still included the ancient ritual of anointing the sovereign with holy oil, the placing of the crown on the monarch's head now occurred in front of a group of leading citizens and peers of the realm. One of the most 'modern' aspects of the coronation was it's live broadcast by television by the BBC. Shortly after the coronation, Elizabeth undertook the first of her numerous royal tours that were to become a feature of her reign.

The queen takes her role as head of the Commonwealth seriously (the word 'British' was dropped from the title in 1948) by making visits to former dominions and colonies. Although most of the Commonwealth countries were independent republics, the Queen remained sovereign of Canada, Australia and New Zealand. At home Elizabeth and Philip – who became known and liked for his outspokenness (if at times he did make the occasional 'gaffe') – spent much of their lives engaged in ceremonial duties, but as British society changed, the monarchy started to seem a little 'remote' and inaccessible.

In 1981 amid a blaze of media frenzy, Prince Charles married Lady Diana Spencer and what looked like a fairytale marriage brought a new popularity to the British monarchy. Their rocky marriage ended in 1992 when the couple separated, but not before a media coverage had laid bare the inner workings of the private lives of the royal family. In the same year, Princess Anne's marriage to Captain Mark Philips also ended, as did Prince Andrew's to Sarah Ferguson. In what the queen described as her 'annus horriblis', Windsor Castle caught fire and when it was revealed that it was uninsured and that the rebuilding costs would be met by the taxpayer, there was outrage: in response, the queen agreed for the first time, to pay income tax.

The young Princess Elizabeth with her parents, 1926.

The coronation in 1953 was watched by some 20 million people on television.

The 1992 fire at Windsor castle ended one of the worst year's in the queen's reign.

Diana, Princess of Wales (1961–97).

Elizabeth II shows no sign of retiring, let alone abdicating.

1952–

The death of Diana, Princess of Wales in 1997 brought more criticism of the Queen – many felt she had not paid her the proper respect – but the death of the Queen Mother aged 101, in 2002 demonstrated that there was still great affection and loyalty for the Crown: thousands queued to pay their respects and file past her coffin laid in state in Westminster Hall. It was clear that in the early years of the 21st century, the British public – and the British media – preferred monarchy to a republic.

In 2002 more than one million people flocked to London to mark the Golden Jubilee of Elizabeth's reign and to celebrate the event. In 'rude health' the queen, now in her 80s, continues to make public appearances and enjoy her passion for horses: she continues to ride regularly, enjoys the annual meetings at Royal Ascot and the Derby at Epsom, and is the breeder and owner of a number of successful racehorses. She is the second-longest reigning British monarch (after Queen Victoria) and the oldest reigning British monarch ever. Her husband, Prince Philip is both the oldest serving spouse and the longest serving consort of a reigning British Monarch.

The past few years have seen some special events and occasions in the life of the Queen and her family. In April 2011 she attended the christening of her first great-grandchild - Savannah, the daughter of Peter and Autumn Phillips. In April 2011, her son, Prince Charles, became Britain's longest-serving heir to the throne. Currently the second-oldest heir apparent, he will become the oldest in 2013. 2011 also saw the eagerly awaited marriage between Prince William and Kate Middleton, a couple whose modern outlook and down-to-earth style have helped boost the popularity of the Royal Family anew.

Historic changes have also been afoot during the past years. Proposals set out in The Succession to the Crown Bill of 2004 would see the rules of British succession changing to absolute primogeniture - by which the oldest child, regardless of gender, would inherit the throne. An agreement was reached in October 2011 that absolute primogeniture would be introduced in the Commonwealth realms at some future date.

2012 will be a very special year for Queen Elizabeth II, and the country as a whole. As only the second monarch to celebrate a Diamond Jubilee, the Queen will be taking an extended visit through England, Scotland, Wales and Ireland, as well as enjoying many other events throughout the year. Then July sees the opening of the London Olympics, with the main Olympic Park to be renamed Queen Elizabeth Olympic Park after the Olympics, and to commemorate her Diamond Jubilee.

SCOTTISH KINGS & QUEENS:

FROM KENNETH MACALPIN TO MARY, QUEEN OF SCOTS

Scotland had an extremely long history and enjoyed independence under its own monarchs until 1603, when Elizabeth I's heir, the Stuart king James VI of Scotland was crowned James I of England thereby uniting the two countries.

Christianity arrived in Scotland at the end of the 4th century after some 1,200 years of pagan Celtic civilisation when St Ninian, an English-born cleric and scholar founded a church at Whithorn in Galloway in the 390s. St Columba, an Irish scholar from Derry, established the monastery at Iona off the west coast of Scotland in the 560s and sent missionaries to convert the Picts and Scots. By the time of Columba's death in 597, Scotland was largely a Christian country.

UNITED SCOTLAND

By this time, Scotland comprised four kingdoms: Dalriada in the west inhabited by Scots from Ireland; a Pictish kingdom in the north; the kingdom of Strathclyde in the southwest, and Bernica (or Lothian) in the east. In the 840s the King of Dalriada, Kenneth MacAlpin (810–58) brought the Picts under his control and created a united country in the north. As well as internal struggles, the first Scottish kings also had to deal with incursions by the English into their lands, and the constant threat of Viking raids. In 1018 Malcolm II (r. 1005–34) overwhelmed a combined Viking and English force that then allowed him to extend his rule over Lothian, with Strathclyde joining the kingdom in 1019.

It was under the rule of Malcolm III, who reigned from 1057–93, that tensions between Scotland and England grew, as English monarchs began to attempt to bring Scotland under its rule. From the 11th century until the 16th century, Scotland struggled to preserve its independence. In 1071–72, William the Conqueror invaded Scotland and compelled Malcolm III to recognize the English king as his overlord. In 1093 Malcolm retaliated and invaded England, but was defeated and killed. Malcolm was succeeded by his brother Donald II (Donald Blane), who was in turn deposed by Duncan II (Malcolm III's son).

During Malcolm III's reign the first castles were built: to begin with these were simple motte-and-bailey castles of raised earth mounds, ditches and wooden defences. By 1100, however, the first stone castle on the shores of Loch Sween in Argyll was well under construction. Malcolm III invaded the northern countries of England five times during his reign in order to annex them to Scotland, and this campaign was continued by his youngest son, David I (r. 1124–53), one of Scotland's greatest early kings. David I was a patron of the church and established several abbeys, notably Dryburgh, Jedburgh, Melrose and Kelso. He introduced feudalism into Scotland, which encouraged several powerful families to settle, including the de Brus (Bruce), the de Bailleuls (Balliols) from Picardy and the FitzAlans from Brittany, whose senior representative became the Hereditary Steward of Scotland and took the name Stewart. (By 1603, the name would be spelled in the French manner, as Stuart, a form that arose after James V of Scotland took French nationality in 1537).

Malcolm III tried to expand his southern borders by invading England.

David I's invasion of England was defeated in 1138 at the Battle of the Standard.

Iona was the first Christian site in Scotland.

THE TWO ALEXANDERS & THE STRUGGLE FOR INDEPENDENCE

In 1138 David I invaded England but was defeated by the English king Stephen at the Battle of the Standard at Northallerton. After David's death in 1154 the struggle against English domination was continued by his successors Malcolm IV and William the Lyon, whose unsuccessful invasion of England in 1174 resulted in his capture by Henry II and the surrender of Scottish independence.

In 1189, however, the English king Richard I recognised Scottish independence in exchange for cash to finance the Third Crusade to the Holy Land. Independent once more, Scotland nevertheless faced constant threat from the Vikings. Alexander II (r.1214-1249) consolidated the peace with England through a treaty with Henry III and married the English king's sister Joan. The ensuing peace with England allowed Alexander to focus on ending the Viking occupation of the Western Isles and parts of the Scottish mainland, and in 1222 he ousted the Vikings from Argyll. In 1237 the Treaty of York agreed the border between Scotland and England, running along the River Tweed and the Cheviot Hills to the Solway Firth, and Alexander also renounced the Scottish claims to the English border counties of Northumberland and Westmoreland.

His planned invasion of the Western Isles, however, came to a halt when Alexander died before the expedition sailed. Succeeded by his son Alexander III, Scotland was victorious at the Battle of Largs on the Firth of Clyde in 1263, when the Viking army led by Haakon IV of Norway was defeated. Three years later, Alexander IIII reclaimed the Western Isles for Scotland. Scotland was heading towards peace and prosperity, when Alexander died suddenly after falling from his horse and down a cliff in 1286. The throne of Scotland was now in the hands of his granddaughter, Margaret, the Maid of Norway, who was just four years old and died on her way back to Scotland.

BALLIOL AND ENGLISH INTERVENTION

After the infant-queen Margaret died, the Scottish nobles could not decide on who should succeed to the throne and turned to Edward I, the English king to act as arbitrator. Edward selected John Balliol, a descendent of David I, but whom the English sensed would do exactly as they demanded – or so they thought. In 1294 Balliol rejected a demand from Edward to join the English on a campaign against France and instead began the 'Auld Alliance' between Scotland and France. Edward was furious and retaliated in 1296 with an invasion of Scotland, deposed Balliol – 'ridding himself of a turd' as Edward put it – and named himself overlord of the kingdom, appointing English nobles backed by an army of occupation to rule Scotland in his name. To add insult to injury, Edward also took the Stone of Scone on which the Scottish kings had sat for their coronations from Scotland to Westminster Abbey.

843–1567

SCOTTISH HEROES: WILLIAM WALLACE AND ROBERT THE BRUCE

The English rule in Scotland was never fully accepted and in 1297 William Wallace, a Scottish patriot of Welsh descent, rose in revolt and defeated the English at Stirling Bridge (1297) before being defeated at Falkirk the following year. For the next seven years Wallace waged a guerrilla campaign against the English until, in 1305, he was betrayed, captured and sent to London. Found guilty of treason, Wallace was hung, drawn and quartered, but his death did not end the Scottish revolt In 1306 Robert the Bruce was crowned at Scone as Robert I. The Bruces had been Lords of Annandale in the Borders since 1120 and a Bruce had lost out in the 'competition' for the crown to Balliol in 1292.

Robert I's coronation enraged Edward I and although ill and close to dying, he again sent an army to Scotland, forcing Robert into hiding on Rathlin Island off the coast of Ireland, while his three brothers were executed and his sister Mary was imprisoned like an animal in a cage that was suspended off the wall of Roxborough Castle for four years. It was at this point that according to legend, Robert took shelter for the night in a cave, where he watched a spider trying over and over again to spin its web until it succeeded. Robert took the lesson to heart: his resolve and his courage were once again restored.

BANNOCKBURN

In 1307 Edward I of England died and Robert recommenced his campaigns against English rule, quickly gathering enough support for the Scots to lay siege to several castles, and gradually driving out many English garrisons by starving them into submission. In 1314 Bruce finally besieged Stirling Castle. The new English king Edward II tried to relieve the siege by sending a huge army that made its camp at Bannockburn, about two miles to the south. On 24 June, the two armies met: Bruce's army was only one-third the size of the English but, by forming 'schiltrons' (rings of men with spears leveled at each point of assault), the Scots repelled the attack and broke the English lines. Amid scenes of bloody chaos, the English soldiers fled the field, taking with the defeated English king with them.

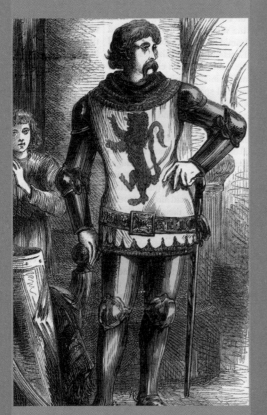

The Scottish hero, Sir William Wallace (1272–1305) led the resistance to English rule imposed by Edward I of England..

Robert Bruce (r. 1306–29) was one of the most successful kings of Scotland and one of the greatest warriors of his time.

Robert the Bruce fighting Henry de Bohun, at Bannockburn, 1314.

Robert II was the first of the Stuart kings of Scotland.

THE DECLARATION OF ARBROATH

After the victory at Bannockburn, Bruce expected the English to quit Scotland and leave the country alone and independent. However, this did not happen, so in 1320 a number of Scottish lords and bishops met in Arbroath to draft an appeal to Pope John XXII insisting on papal recognition of Scotland's independence. While this was followed by a truce between Bruce and Edward II in 1323, neither succeeded in preventing continued warfare. On the accession of Edward III in England in 1327, Robert the Bruce launched an invasion to force the new king to recognise Scotland's independence, which came about the following year in the Treaty of Edinburgh which was ratified by the English as the Treaty of Northampton. Robert the Bruce was finally and formally recognised as King of Scotland. By this time Bruce was already seriously ill and the next year, 1329, he was dead. He had long wanted to go on Crusade, so after his death, his heart was removed from his body and taken by Sir James Douglas with an escort of knights to carry it to the Holy Land. The group only got as far as Spain, where it was said it was carried aloft into battle against the Moors. Sir James died in the battle, but it is said that Robert the Bruce's heart was returned to Scotland and buried at Melrose Abbey.

DARK DAYS: THE FIRST STEWART KINGS

The death of Robert the Bruce in 1329 ushered in a period of dark and troubled times for Scotland. As his five-year-old son David II was crowned at Scone, the Balliol family were in league with Edward III and began their campaign to reclaim the throne. So troubled were the Scottish lords that they sent David and his child bride Joan (Edward III's own sister) to safety in France in 1333. They returned in 1340, and in 1346 David led his army to defeat by the English at Durham. Wounded in the head David was held prisoner in England for 11 years. Released in 1357 after a substantial ransom had been paid, David died childless in 1371 and was succeeded by Robert Stewart.

Robert Stewart (r. 1371–90), known as 'Old Blearie' because of his bloodshot eyes, was 55 when he became king (as Robert II) and was already an experienced and shrewd politician who was dedicated to the advancement of his own family. He is said to have fathered at least 21 children, both legitimate and otherwise, which ensured the Stewart succession. He, and his disabled son Robert III (r. 1390–1406) who became king in 1390, had to deal with renewed tensions with the English as well as fighting between the Scottish clans. Robert III's own brothers, Robert, Duke of Albany who

843–1567

oversaw rule in the Lowlands, and Alexander 'the Wolf of Badenoch', who held the north in his power, were also vying for control over the ineffective Robert III who, in his own words described himself as 'the worst of kings and the most wretched of men in the whole realm' and allegedly remarked that he should be buried under a dunghill. Matters came to a head in 1399 when a royal council appointed Robert III's eldest son David as 'lieutenant' of Scotland. Albany was soon on the move and imprisoned David at Falkirk who was left, according to rumour, to starve to death in solitary confinement while Albany ruled as regent. Hoping to save James, his remaining son and heir, from Albany's grasp, Robert III sent him to France, but the 12-year-old was captured by the English off Flamborough Head and held prisoner for 18 years while the English tried in vain to take control of Scotland.

Albany died in 1420 and four years later, James I, aged 30, returned to Scotland accompanied by his English wife Lady Jane Beaufort, and promptly executed many of Albany's remaining family, also 'dispatching' a number of clan chiefs whom he saw as a threat. Determined to reform Scotland, James increased taxes, and banned fishing out of season – and football in any season. These reforms, along with other harsh measures, made him unpopular: in 1437 his uncle the Earl of Athol arranged for the king's murder in the royal apartments at Perth Castle. The fleeing king was stabbed to death in a sewer under the floor.

Born in 1394, James I was king of Scotland from 1406, but he was imprisoned by the English for 18 years until the Scots agreed to pay a ransom of £40,000 to release him. He returned to his kingdom in 1424.

FROM JAMES II TO JAMES V

Like James I, the kings of Scotland from James II to James V, all succeeded to the throne as children and all died violent deaths. James II (r. 1437–60), known as 'Fiery Face' (and famous for banning golf) succeeded his father in 1437 aged just six years old and was the titular ruler of an unruly kingdom. When he came of age he immediately set about exerting control over his nobles but could only break the power of the Earls of Douglas by treacherously killing the eighth earl before defeating the ninth in battle and using his parliament to confiscate their estates. In 1449 James married Marie of Gueldres (a province in Arnheim, in the lower Rhine region) who brought with her an arsenal of new artillery that enthralled the king: it's possible that she brought the famous 'Mons Meg' canon with her to Scotland. In 1460 James was besieging the English at Roxborough Castle when he attempted to impress his queen by setting off a canon, but it exploded and killed him. Marie was clearly made of stout stuff: she immediately took charge and saw the siege through to its successful conclusion.

James III (r. 1451–88) was only nine when his succeeded his father, so a regency council ruled Scotland until he took matters into his own hands in the 1470s. Interested in the arts, astrology and alchemy James was also greedy for money, had a liking for low-born 'entertainers' and was intent on peace with England – a stance that angered many nobles as well as his own brothers John and Alexander. In 1479 James had his brothers arrested: John died in prison, apparently having bled to death in the bath, while Alexander escaped down a rope and fled to France. It was left to the disaffected Scottish nobles to deal with the problem and in 1482, James III was taken prisoner at Lauder by the Earl of Angus. He survived, but in 1485 another uprising occurred, in which his son and heir James IV was involved. At the Battle of Sauchieburn in 1488, the fleeing James III was killed, possibly by accident: his son was horrified and wore an iron chain around his waist next to his skin for the rest of his life as a mark of remorse.

James IV (r. 1488–1513) was 15 when he became king and became one of the most popular of the Stewart monarchs. Handsome, brave, and intelligent, he spoke seven languages including Gaelic, sponsored the arts and created the Scottish navy which included the *Great Michael*, the largest warship afloat. He was also interested in science: he encouraged his alchemist's attempts to fly with wings off the battlements of Stirling Castle (he landed in a dung heap) and paid volunteers to let him extract their teeth. As well as sponsoring the first Scottish university medical school at Aberdeen in 1495, James IV also approved the establishment of Scotland's first printing press under Andrew Myllar in 1507. In 1502 James signed a treaty of perpetual peace with Henry VII of England and the following year married Henry's daughter, Margaret Tudor. James was 30, his bride just 13 and the new Scottish queen soon discovered the nursery at Stirling Castle already occupied by seven of her husband's illegitimate children borne by a succession of mistresses. Few of their own children

843–1567

survived, but their great-grandson James VI of Scotland eventually inherited both the Scottish and English thrones. When Henry VIII invaded France in 1513, James IV renewed the 'Auld Alliance' with France and invaded England: his army of 20,000 men were defeated at Flodden and the king, and a great number of Scottish nobles were killed. James IV's body was eventually embalmed and sent to London where some years later it was said that workmen cut off his head and used it as a football.

The new king, James V (r. 1513–42), was even younger than his predecessors when he inherited the throne, at just 17 months old. Once again Scotland was ruled by a regency under the Duke of Albany (a grandson of James II, who returned from France). These early years saw a power struggle between the regency and James' mother, who after being widowed, married Archibald Douglas, Earl of Angus and who effectively held James prisoner for three years.

James escaped his imprisonment in 1528 and, taking control for himself, he proved to be a competent if ruthless ruler. But, desperately short of money, he aroused anger by increasing taxes and to further boost the royal coffers, he seized the Angus lands. Angus's sister Janet was burned to death on trumped-up charges of plotting to poison him. James was also determined to bring the Armstrongs of Liddesdale in the Borders to heel (they were notorious raiders and rustlers) and had many of the family hanged as outlaws. In 1537 James concluded a marriage alliance with France: his wife Madeleine was the daughter of Francois I but she died shortly after. Quickly James re-married, again to a French bride, Mary of Guise-Lorraine. She bore James two sons but they both died in 1541. The following year Mary was pregnant again. In the meantime, James was occupied with fighting the English. On 24 November 1542 the Scots were routed at the Battle of Solway Moss near Gretna and two weeks later James V died at his palace at Falkland: his death took place just a few days after the birth of his heir, the ill-fated Mary, Queen of Scots.

Before he died, he was reputed to have said of his dynasty, 'It came wi' a lass, it'll gang wi' a lass'. The Stuarts originally claimed the throne through Robert the Bruce's daughter Majorie, and the line died out in 1714 with the death of Queen Anne.

James IV was a Renaissance prince, who did a great deal to encourage learning in Scotland.

James V left only a six-day old baby girl as his legitimate heir, but his illegitimate son James Earl of Moray (1531–70) proved to be an invaluable advisor to his half-sister Mary Queen of Scots.

1542–1567

Queen of Scotland and briefly Queen of France, Mary was just six days old when she succeeded to the throne in 1542. The following year it was decided that she would marry the young son of Henry VIII, the future king Edward VI, but in the meantime, England continued to attack its northern neighbour. When Edward became king in 1547, France landed 6,000 troops in Scotland and declared war on England. In the ensuing power struggle, Mary was betrothed to the French dauphin whom she married in 1558. Shortly after her marriage, the English queen Mary I died and the young Scottish queen saw the opportunity to press her own claim on the English throne. She was, however, passed over in favour of her cousin, Elizabeth I but nevertheless pursued her claim, which was strengthened (militarily at least) when Mary's husband became Francois II, King of France in 1559 and she, Queen of France. While Mary reigned in France, her mother Marie of Guise ruled Scotland as regent, but Mary's reign in France would be brief: Francois died in 1560 and she returned to Scotland in 1561.

Back home, Mary found that the Reformation, which was both political and religious in nature. It had begun in the 1540s, had turned Scotland from a Catholic country into a Protestant nation. It had ended the 'Auld Alliance' with France and brought Scotland so close to England that union was almost inevitable. Chief architect of the Scottish Reformation was the fiery priest John Knox, who had been influenced by John Calvin of Geneva. In 1559 Knox had returned from exile to Scotland and the following year the Scottish parliament has decided that Protestantism was to be the nation's religion. The queen, however, was a staunch Catholic and as such, she was a thorn in the side of both Knox and her cousin, Elizabeth I.

In 1565 Mary married her cousin, Henry Stuart, Lord Darnley but before long seems to have fallen in love with her secretary David Rizzio who, before her eyes, was murdered. Stabbed and clinging to Mary's skirts, and begging for his life, the Italian was dragged away and killed on the stairs at Holyroodhouse in 1566. In June that year Mary gave birth to a son and heir James, and in February 1567 Darnley was himself murdered. At two o'clock in the morning, a house in Edinburgh where he had gone to recover from illness (possibly syphilis) was blown up by a huge explosion. Barrels of gunpowder had been packed into the cellars, and the bodies of Darnley and his valet were found in the garden, although it was clear they had been strangled before the explosion.

1542–1567

Suspicion centred on James Hepburn, Earl of Bothwell (to whom Mary had been showing some attention) and whether Mary knew about Darnley's death in advance, no-one knows for sure. The so-called 'Casket Letters' from the queen to Bothwell which were supposed to prove her guilt, disappeared in the reign of James VI and may well have been forgeries to be used as 'anti-Mary' propaganda by her enemies. With Darnley out of the way, Bothwell took his chance: in April 1567 he carried Mary off to Dunbar Castle where allegedly, he raped her. Nevertheless, in May, Mary was married to Bothwell at Holyroodhouse in a low-key Protestant ceremony. It was all too much even for Mary's Catholic sympathisers: in June an alliance of nobles led by James Douglas, Earl of Morton confronted Mary and Bothwell at Carberry Hill, east of Edinburgh. Mary's army deserted and she surrendered before the first blow had even been struck. Bothwell fled to Orkney (and would ultimately die insane in Norway) while Mary was taken to Edinburgh where a mob screamed at her captors to 'burn the whore'. She was taken as prisoner to an island in Loch Leven and in July 1567, was forced to abdicate in favour of her baby son. Her half-brother, James Stewart, Earl of Moray was nominated as regent.

After a failed attempted to escape when she disguised herself as a washerwoman (her identity was evidently betrayed by her soft, white hands), Mary finally broke out of her island prison in 1568 and raised an army with the support of the Hamiltons, the Gordons and the Campbells. She was defeated at the Battle of Langside by the regent Moray.

Mary fled to England begging Elizabeth I's protection. She was still only 25 years old and would now spend the remaining 19 years of her life as a prisoner in England. Mary and Elizabeth never met, and while the English queen was repeatedly urged to execute Mary (who was the focus of many Catholic plots against Elizabeth) this did not happen until 1587. In this year, Mary's involvement in Anthony Babington's assassination plot against Elizabeth created such ill feeling that the English queen was compelled to act. Mary was beheaded at Fotheringhay Castle in Northamptonshire in 1587. It took three strokes of the axe to remove her head. Her son James VI of Scotland, who had been crowned in Scotland in 1567 and would be crowned James I of England in 1603, had not moved to help his mother in any way, and only had her body transferred to a tomb in Westminster Abbey in 1612.

Henry Stuart, Lord Darnley (1545–67) was Mary's cousin. Three years younger than Mary, handsome and unpopular with the other Scottish lords, Darnley was jealous of Mary's flirtation with her secretary David Rizzio.

Mary Queen of Scots spent 19 years imprisoned by Elizabeth I. She was eventually convicted of treason after her involvement in the Babington Plot. She was executed at Fotheringhay Castle aged 44.

INDEX

BIBLIOGRAPHY

Andrew, A (1994) Kings and Queens of England and Scotland Marshall Cavendish
Ashley, M (1999) Mammoth Book of Kings and Queens Constable
Cavendish, R and Leahy, P (2006) Kings and Queens David and Charles
Cheshire, P (2006) Kings and Queens, Chiefs and Rulers: A Source Book Flame Tree
Delderfield, E (1998) Kings and Queens of Great Britain David and Charles
Douglas, M and Humphreys, G (1999) Collins Fact Book: Kings and Queens of Britain Collins
Elton, G (1991) Life Under the Tudors Routledge
Frazer, A (ed) (1993) The Lives of the Kings and Queens of England Wiedenfeld
Grant, N (1999) Collins Gem: Kings and Queens Harper Collins
Lambert, D and Gray, R (1991) Kings and Queens Harper Collins
Newman, P.A (1990) A Companion to the English Civil Wars Oxford
Stewart, R (1990) Monarchs of Scotland Moffat
Williamson, D (1996) Kings and Queens of Britain Webb and Bower

PICTURE CREDITS